Cyclopedia of
Young Adult Authors

Cyclopedia of
Young Adult Authors

Volume 1

Joan Abelove–Esther Forbes

From
The Editors of Salem Press

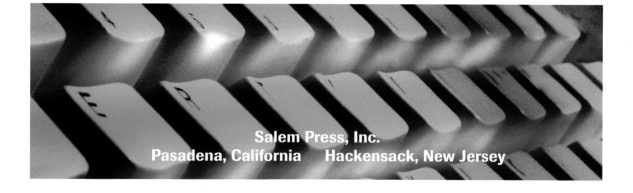

Salem Press, Inc.
Pasadena, California   Hackensack, New Jersey

Editor in Chief: Dawn P. Dawson
Project Editors: Kenneth T. Burles
R. Kent Rasmussen
Acquisitions Editor: Mark Rehn
Production Editor: Cynthia Beres
Photograph Editor: Philip Bader
Design: Moritz Design, Pasadena, California
Page Layout and Graphics: James Hutson
Assistant Editor: Andrea E. Miller
Editorial Intern: Heather Pistole

Library of Congress Cataloging-in-Publication Data

Cyclopedia of young adult authors / from the editors of Salem Press.
   p. cm.
  Includes bibliographical references and index.
  ISBN 1-58765-206-4 (set : alk. paper) — ISBN 1-58765-207-2 (vol. 1 : alk. paper) —
ISBN 1-58765-208-0 (vol. 2 : alk. paper) — ISBN 1-58765-209-9 (vol. 3 : alk. paper)
  1. Young adult literature, American—Dictionaries. 2. Young adult literature, English—Dictionaries. 3. Authors, American—Biography—Dictionaries. 4. Authors, English—Biography—Dictionaries. I. Salem Press.
  PS490.C93 2005
  810.9'9283'03—dc22

                                                 2004027668

First Printing
Printed in Canada

Contents

Volume 1

E

F

Publisher's Note

Authors always have written books that appealed to young adult readers, but it was not until the mid-twentieth century that a group of authors began to target young adults as the audience for their books. S. E. Hinton, one of those writers, commented that she set out to write the kind of books she would have liked to have read when she was a young adult. In fact, her first novel, *The Outsiders*, published in 1967, was written while she was still in high school. Since that time, a group of authors has emerged who write for the young adult reader. Like Hinton, some deal with the gritty realities of young adults' lives. Others chose to write science fiction and fantasy tales that appeal to young adults and deal with issues that concern them. Yet other authors write mystery or thriller stories. While all this writing that targets the younger reader has been taking place, there remain classic novels written for adults that continue to appeal to the interests of young adults and that have found a permanent home in the school curriculum. What has evolved is a body of literature written for young adults or appealing to young adults that has true literary merit.

Cyclopedia of Young Adult Authors offers young adult readers a way to appreciate the lives and works of this special group of fiction writers. It began its life as a database on authors for NoveList, the subscription reader's advisory service available through many school and public libraries. From the basic appreciation of two hundred and fifty-one authors' lives and works, the editors have constructed a multifaceted reference book for young adults to use in the library. The addition of informative sidebars explaining concepts, terms, awards, professions, places, and other topics encountered in the author essays broadens the reader's experience. Adding photos, graphics, and other illustration in a colorful page design creates an interactive book that attracts students working on class assignments, needing general reference on authors, or simply browsing in the library.

Each author article contains essential information about the author:

- Author's name
- Birthdate and place, and, when appropriate, death date and place
- Official or useful Web site when available
- Principal works of young adult fiction
- Opening paragraph summarizing what makes the author noteworthy and interesting to young adults
- Discussion of the author's life and works, giving the young adult reader an appreciation for the author and piquing interest in reading the works
- Signed with an academic, librarian, or independent scholar contributor's byline

Interesting topics that appear in the text have been selected for discussion in two sidebars per article. No topic is covered more than once and indexing provides access to the sidebars throughout the book. Included are:

- Description of awards such as the Carnegie Medal, Newbery Medal, ALA Best Books for Young Adults and many more prizes and honors
- Explanation of such things as a Rhodes Scholar, Fulbright Scholarship, magistrate, technical writer, or the American Library Association
- Description of places such as the Brazilian rain forest, Wales, Jamaica, or Ethiopia

Colorful illustration to hold young adult readers' interest includes:

- Maps locating a place on the globe
- Color photographs of such places as Oxford University, Royal Shakespeare Theatre, and the House of the Seven Gables
- Logos, medals, or other graphic elements

We wish to thank all of the writers who contributed to this book for helping readers appreciate the lives and works of the young adult authors profiled here.

How To Use This Book

Table of Contents: Readers can use the Table of Contents to locate an author by looking for the author's last name alphabetically. The Contents page will direct users to the opening page of the author article.

Web Sites: We have identified Web sites that contain additional useful information about one or more authors. They appear in the header of each author article. Web sites can change or be discontinued. We hope we have chosen stable sites that will continue to be available to readers.

Sidebar Flags: In the margins, readers will encounter colorful arrows showing a page number. Each arrow corresponds to a word, term, or title that is also highlighted in nearby text in the same color. The number directs the reader to the page on which a sidebar explaining that word, term, or title appears. The sidebar may appear on the same page, a facing page, or a page in another volume of the book.

Illustrations: At the back of each volume the sources of the illustrations are credited.

Awards: At the back of volume three is a list of some of the many awards, prizes, and honors given to writers of young adult literature.

Subject Index: At the back of each volume, readers will find a Subject Index to all three volumes of the book helping them locate an author, book titles discussed in text, sidebar topics, and terms that help readers identify the authors that interest them.

Contributors

Jan Allister
St. Olaf College

Philip Bader
Independent Scholar

Henry J. Baron
Calvin College

David Barratt
Independent Scholar

Kathleen M. Bartlett
RSK Assessments, Inc.

Kevin J. Bochynski
Salem State College

Kristin C. Brunnemer
University of California, Riverside

Faith Hickman Brynie
Independent Scholar

Ken Burles
Independent Scholar

Susan Butterworth
Salem State College

Ann M. Cameron
Indiana University, Kokomo

Anita Price Davis
Converse College

Mary Virginia Davis
University of California, Davis

Deborah DePiero
University of Rhode Island

Margaret A. Dodson
Independent Scholar

Stefan Dziemianowicz
Independent Scholar

Thomas R. Feller
Independent Scholar

Lisa Rowe Fraustino
Eastern Connecticut State University

Sheldon Goldfarb
University of British Columbia

Emma Harris
Walters State Community College

Joan Hope
Independent Scholar

Mary Hurd
East Tennessee State University

Grace Jasmine
Independent Scholar

Jeffry Jensen
Independent Scholar

Leslie Ellen Jones
Independent Scholar

Fiona Kelleghan
University of Miami

Cassandra Kircher
Elon University

Grove Koger
Boise Public Library, Idaho

Leon Lewis
Appalachian State University

Bernadette Flynn Low
*Community College of Baltimore County —
Dundalk*

R. C. Lutz
CII-ME

Kay Moore
California State University, Sacramento

Bernard E. Morris
Independent Scholar

R. Kent Rasmussen
Independent Scholar

Rosemary M. Canfield Reisman
Charleston Southern University

Angela M. Salas
Southeast Missouri State University

Alexa L. Sandmann
University of Toledo

Carroll Dale Short
Independent Scholar

R. Baird Shuman
*University of Illinois at Urbana—
Champaign*

Amy Sisson
Independent Scholar

Brian Stableford
King Alfred's College

Joshua Stein
Los Medanos College

Richard Tuerk
Texas A&M University — Commerce

Raymond Wilson
Fort Hays State University

Sharon K. Wilson
Fort Hays State University

Cyclopedia of
Young Adult Authors

Joan Abelove

Born: January 14, 1945; Sarasota, Florida

www.penguinputnam.com/Author/
AuthorFrame?0000030814

Joan Abelove is known for her psychologically honest and emotionally moving novels for young adults.

p.2 As a graduate student, she went to the Amazon **rain forest** in 1972 to study interactions among mothers and infants, gathering material for her doctoral dissertation in clinical psychology. However, while she was there, she decided that what she really wanted to study was anthropology. Upon her return to New York two years later, she switched departments and completed her doctorate in anthropology. After teaching for several years, she turned p.3 to **technical writing** as a profession. Although it was to be her second published book, *Saying It Out Loud* was the first work of fiction that she completed. She began it in 1991 while attending a workshop on writing for children.

Abelove wanted to write a book about her experiences living in the **rain forest**. She especially wanted to write about a young Brazilian woman who had become her friend. She was anxious to explore what human emotional force draws people to each other as friends, despite the differences that may be caused by language, culture, and history. However, writing this story did not come easily; she had many false starts. It was only after she found the right voice to tell her story that she could complete the novel. p.2

Narrated by the teenage Alicia of the fictional Isabo people of the Amazon Basin, *Go and Come Back* opens with the line, "Two old white ladies came

TITLES

Go and Come Back, 1998

Saying It Out Loud, 1999

to our village late one day. . . ." Alicia perceives these women as "old," but the women are actually only in their twenties. This is one of many humorous details in Abelove's treatment of two clashing cultures. Through the viewpoint of Alicia, readers can see American ways through fresh eyes, while learning sympathetically about another, very different way of life. The book explores the views of sex and marriage held by Alicia's own people. Isabo words color Alicia's speech and reflect her people's perceptions of the world. For example, the Isabo have no word exactly equivalent to "goodbye." They say "Catanhue" when they part, meaning something similar to "go and come back"—which gives Abelove's novel its title.

Those who read *Saying It Out Loud* expecting another exotic setting will be in for a surprise. Abelove again uses a spirited heroine with a distinctive voice including humor, but this narrator is a sixteen-year-old American high school student whose mother is dying of a brain

Brazilian Rain Forest

The Amazon River Basin contains the world's largest rain forest and about a fifth of the world's freshwater. The wet, humid climate encourages growth of more species of plants and animals than anywhere else on earth. The forested area acts as the earth's lungs, absorbing carbon dioxide and releasing oxygen into the air. A thick canopy of trees covers most of the basin, and light does not reach the floor of the basin. Therefore, there is little plant life on the ground. Instead, plants grow on the trees. Many plants in the rain forest are used to develop medicines.

As population growth threatens the rain forest with development, the world's biological diversity is also threatened. The financial rewards of mining minerals and harvesting lumber attract business, as does the promise of new farm land created by clearing patches of the rain forest. Large areas of rain forest have been burned to clear the land. However, the soil in the rain forest is not rich and will not support farming without allowing time for nature to restore the environmental balance.

Technical Writer

A technical writer is someone who makes difficult instructions or definitions easier to understand. These writers work for companies that produce products we use everyday, such as radios and television sets. They provide us with the instructions needed to install the device and to operate it. Today, many technical writers are employed by computer software companies. They try to explain how to use the software we load into our computers so we can perform certain tasks. What they write is published in technical manuals or in on-screen help files.

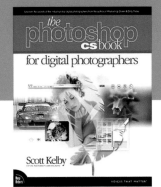

tumor. With the help of friends, Mindy comes to grips with her loss and her regrets. Again Abelove works with the theme of respect for differences, this time the clash being the more familiar conflict between mothers and adolescent daughters.

Abelove's books have received numerous honors. Both *Go and Come Back* and *Saying It Out Loud* were named **Best Books for Young Adults** by the **American Library Association** and **Best Books for the Teen Age** by the **New York Public Library**. Abelove has also published short stories in anthologies and continues to make her living as a technical writer. She resides in New York City with her husband and son.

– Lisa Rowe Fraustino

p.480
p.156
p.45

Douglas Adams

Born: March 11, 1952; Cambridge, England
Died: May 11, 2001; Santa Barbara, California
www.douglasadams.com

Douglas Adams was, along with Terry Pratchett, one of the pioneers of modern British humorous science fiction, in which the fantastic elements of the plot and the possibilities for endless alternative realities offer opportunities for social satire. Adams claimed Lewis Carroll and P. G. Wodehouse as his literary heroes; his own work united the scientific and mathematical playfulness of Carroll with the sheer social farce of Wodehouse, the creator of Bertie Wooster and Jeeves.

Born in Cambridge, England, Adams attended the prestigious **Cambridge University**, majoring in English. Cambridge and **Oxford University** were breeding grounds for British humorists during the 1960's and 1970's and produced such comics as the members of Monty Python's Flying Circus. Like many of these comics, Adams was an enthusiastic member of the Cambridge Footlights theatrical club. Again like many Footlights members before him, Adams wound up working for the **British Broadcasting Corporation** (BBC), in his case as a script editor for the long-running science-fiction television series *Dr. Who.*

Adams often said that the idea for his breakthrough Hitchhiker's Guide to the Galaxy series came to him one night as he lay drunk in a field outside Innsbruck, Austria, led there by a popular "Hitchhiker's" travel guide to Europe. Looking up at the stars, he thought, "Why not a hitchhiker's guide to the galaxy?" He used his contacts in the BBC to present the idea for a **radio series** recount-

p.5

p.173

p.6

p.564

Cambridge University

One of the oldest universities in England, the University of Cambridge was founded in 1209 by a number of students from Oxford. By the late 1800's enrollment had increased, and in 1873 the university opened the first college for women. The university consists of 19 colleges for men and 3 for women. In addition, three men's colleges began admitting women after 1971. Among those who have studied at Cambridge are many famous people from all fields. Cambridge boasts more Nobel Prize winners than any other institution, including mathematician and philosopher Bertrand Russell, DNA scientists Frances Crick and James Watson, and chemist Dorothy Crowfoot Hodgkin.

ing the misadventures of Arthur Dent, a normal human being who abruptly discovers that his friend Ford Prefect is an extraterrestrial alien who became stranded on Earth while doing research for a book called *The Hitchhiker's Guide to the Galaxy*. Moreover, Earth is about to be destroyed to make way for a hyperspace bypass. Ford is about to grab a lift on the Vogon spaceship sent to do the job and will take Arthur with him.

Thus Arthur begins his picaresque adventures on the spaceship *Heart of Gold*, powered by the Infinite Improbability Drive. He is accompanied by Ford, the two-headed Zaphod Beeblebrox, Zaphod's girlfriend Trillian, and the interminably depressed robot Marvin. Side effects of the Infinite Improbability Drive land the travelers in a series of predicaments throughout time and space, during which, among other things, it is revealed that Earth is, in fact, one large laboratory experiment being run by a group of white mice attempting to discover the answer to "life, the universe, and everything." Actually, they already know the answer—42—but now they are trying to figure out exactly what the question is.

Despite its low-budget beginnings, the radio series was so popular that Pan Books in Britain suggested to Adams that a novelization might sell well. p.105 The popularity of the novels in both Britain and the United States led to several sequel novels and a BBC television series. In 1984, Adams became the youngest author to be awarded a **Golden Pan**, which he would win an additional two times for other works. He also was nominated for the **Best of Young British Novelists Award.** Adams was working on a screenplay for a movie version of his series when he died unexpectedly of a heart attack in 2001.

After the *Hitchhiker* series, Adams created another series based on detective Dirk Gently, whose cases explore the worlds of myth and the occult in much the same way that the *Hitchhiker* series explored the worlds of science—that is, with liberal doses of absurdity.

– Leslie Ellen Jones

The BBC

The British Broadcasting Corporation is publicly financed and originally had a monopoly on radio and television broadcasting in Great Britain. In 1952, the Independent Television Authority eliminated the BBC's exclusive right to broadcast television, and local radio stations were authorized in the 1970's. While a monopoly, the BBC was able to broadcast without commercial interruptions. It was responsible for many respected television and radio programs and became known worldwide for the quality of its productions. Advances in broadcasting have enabled the BBC to broadcast in many countries other than Great Britain. BBC America, for example, now broadcasts British programming in the United States on stations across the country.

Richard Adams

Born: May 9, 1920; Newbury, Berkshire, England
www.fantasticfiction.co.uk/authors/
Richard_Adams.htm

There were stories about talking animals long before **Richard Adams** began to write *Watership Down*, but none ever became such a worldwide best-seller. Adams knows how to write suspense, how to portray steadfast loyalty to the point of sacrifice, and how to show the countryside from a rabbit's point of view, which is very different from that of a human. His dialogue is often funny, and everything except the rabbits' ability to speak is realistic. Readers of all ages continue to love *Watership Down*, which won the **Guardian Award** and the **Carnegie Medal**.

p.42

Born in southern England, Adams grew up loving the English countryside. He was the son of a country doctor, who would later make a brief appearance as the shy "Dr. Adams" near the end of *Watership Down*. After World War II, Adams worked in the national government's Department of the Environment. He loved literature and often drove his daughters to see plays at the **Royal Shakespeare Theatre** in Stratford-on-Avon. That journey took hours, and Adams would tell his daughters stories about the rabbits and other animals of the Berkshire Downs, where he owned a weekend cottage. His daughters insisted that he write down his tales, and he eventually

p.8

TITLES

Watership Down, 1972

Shardik, 1974

The Plague Dogs, 1977

Royal Shakespeare Theatre

Located in Shakespeare's birthplace of Stratford-on-Avon, The Royal Shakespeare Theatre is home to the Royal Shakespeare Company, one of the best known theater companies in the world. The first performance in the Memorial Theatre was held in 1878. The original building was destroyed by fire in 1926 and was replaced by the Shakespeare Memorial Theatre in 1932. From that time on, the Company developed a reputation as the home of the finest Shakespearean actors, and it gained world renown. In 1960, director Peter Hall founded the Royal Shakespeare Company, and one year later the Memorial Theatre was renamed the Royal Shakespeare Theatre. Since that time, the Company has also performed modern works and classics by dramatists in addition to Shakespeare's works.

transformed them into the novel *Watership Down*, which he finished in the mid-1960's. More than twenty publishers rejected the book; most thought it was a children's book and that it was far too long a book to fit into that genre. However, Adams never gave up and eventually sold his **manuscript** to the small London publisher Rex Collings. Since the book came out in 1972, it has sold tens of millions of copies.

p.620

Watership Down is an amazingly exciting story. It begins in a rabbit warren, in which the runt Fiver has visions of the future and warns his brother Hazel that a terrible catastrophe is coming. Hazel leads eleven rabbits away, including brave Bigwig, dashing Dandelion, and clever Blackberry. Hazel gradually becomes their "Chief Rabbit" despite his doubts and fears. He leads them through a variety of dangers, following Fiver's promise that they will make a home on a high hill called Watership Down. Along the way, the rabbits almost die in another warren that is bizarrely cursed, they befriend a wild gull named Kehaar, and they battle their worst enemy, the enormous, ruthless General Woundwort.

Adams's next novel, *Shardik*, is about a gigantic, godlike bear and a man named Keldek who rises from a poor fisherman to become the ruler of the Bekla Empire. This is a novel for adults, but many teenagers may enjoy Keldek's special connection to the bear.

Adams's third novel, *The Plague Dogs*, is more widely read. Brave dog Rowf escapes a horrible laboratory for **animal experimentation** with his pal, the terrier Snitter. They escape onto the bleak hills of northern England during a fierce winter and survive, just barely, with the help of a wild fox. A rascally newspaperman, Digby Driver, prints the story that the two starving dogs are carrying bubonic plague. By the time Driver learns the truth, the dogs are fleeing for their lives. The novel is filled with sour humor, though adults are more likely to appreciate Adams's satiric attacks on the English government, the news media, and abusers of laboratory animals everywhere. Younger readers may skip through these sections and fall in love with the dogs as they search for a kind new owner.

p.9

– Fiona Kelleghan

Animal Experimentation

Animals are often used by the scientific community for research in laboratories. The research may be related to diseases that infect humans or to test the safety of cosmetics or skin ointments. Animal rights activists have challenged the necessity of using animals for this purpose. The argument against the use of animals in research states that animals have the right to live free of human interference. Activists also protest the cruelty, suffering, and pain caused by testing on animals. Animals used in research may be acquired from shelters and the pet industry. The main organizations opposing the use of animals in research are People for the Ethical Treatment of Animals (PETA), the New England Vivesection Society (NEAVS), and the Animal Liberation Front (ALF). There are also those who defend the right to use animals for research. The National Association for Biomedical Research (NABR) and the Incurably Ill for Animal Research (IIFAR) are foremost among them.

C. S. Adler

Born: February 23, 1932; Long Island, New York

www.c-s-adler.com

Carole S. Adler began writing full time in 1979, when her first book, *The Magic of the Glits*, fulfilled her lifelong dream of becoming a published novelist. She continued to write for both children and young adults, building her novels around value-related themes such as the importance of family and friendships, nurturing others, integrity, and honesty. She wants her readers to rate good character above superficial values such as appearance.

While a middle school English teacher, Adler developed insights into the characters, problems, and needs of emerging adolescents. She communicates those insights through realistically drawn young adult characters who work to solve the problems of growing up that ring true to her readers. In *Winning*, for example, thirteen-year-old Vicky must juggle the demands of intense sports competition, a crumbling friendship, and an **ethical** dilemma involving cheating. Vicky maintains her integrity and earns the respect of others, enhancing her own self-confidence in the process—a recurring theme in many of Adler's books.

Adler's characters must often deal with problematic and flawed adults. They remain hopeful in

p.10

Ethics

Ethics is the part of philosophy that deals with questions about the nature and source of right and wrong, good and evil, and what should and should not be done. Your school may have a code of behavior that helps define your ethical behavior.

the face of obstacles, and know that relationships can be repaired. In *Roadside Valentine*, for example, high school senior Jamie Landes strives to communicate with his highly critical father. In *The Shell Lady's Daughter*, fourteen-year-old Kelly struggles to meet the needs of her sick mother while establishing her own independence.

Adler believes she has been fortunate in her life. Successful not only as a writer but also as a wife, mother, and educator, she began as a lonely, shy child. However she felt much loved by her mother, grandmother, and an aunt who lived with her family. Her parents divorced when she was eleven, and she learned independence despite her timidity. Blessed with a strong marriage spanning five decades, she had three sons, losing one tragically in his adulthood. She wrote her most successful novel, *Ghost Brother*, after her son died. Its title character, a fifteen-year old boy who returns as a spirit to guide his little brother, is based on her

The Society of Children's Book Writers and Illustrators

This professional organization was founded in Los Angeles in 1971 by a group of writers for children. It has become an organization with more than 19,000 members worldwide. The SCBWI provides a network for writers, illustrators, editors, publishers, agents, librarians, teachers, and booksellers who are committed to literature for young people. It sponsors annual conferences and events worldwide to spread information about the art and business of writing and selling illustrated children's books. In addition, the SCBWI presents the annual Golden Kite Award for the best illustrated childrens fiction and nonfiction books.

son as he was at that age. The book mirrors her perception of reality, for she believes that her son appeared to her in the flesh and spoke in his own voice for about a year after he died. Otherwise, Adler says that little of her work is autobiographical. She sees herself as an empathic person, and most of her story ideas come not from her own life, but from the lives of others.

C. S. Adler's first published book, *Magic of the Glits*, tells of a boy's sympathy for an orphan girl. It won the Golden Kite Award of the **Society of Children's Book Writers and Illustrators** in 1979 and the **William Allen White Award** in 1982.

p.11
p.111

– Faith Hickman Brynie

Louisa May Alcott

Born: November 29, 1832; Germantown, Pennsylvania
Died: March 6, 1888; Boston, Massachusetts

www.louisamayalcott.org/louisamaytext.html

The second daughter of the famous Transcendentalist philosopher Bronson Alcott, **Louisa May Alcott** grew up in a household short on cash but long on ideas. For most of her childhood, the family lived in Concord, Massachusetts, and Alcott and her three sisters—Anna, Elizabeth, and May—were educated at home. Like all of the Alcotts, Louisa was a supporter of progressive social issues such as woman **p.14** **suffrage**, coeducation, and the abolition of slavery. The Alcotts moved in an intellectual circle that included writers Ralph Waldo Emerson, Henry David Thoreau, and Nathaniel Hawthorne. Louisa spent some time as a teenager tutoring Emerson's daughter Ellen, and this led her to become a teacher at the age of eighteen. She nursed her sister Elizabeth during a long and ultimately fatal illness. When the Civil War broke out in 1861, she also served as a nurse tending wounded Union soldiers until she herself succumbed to typhoid fever. Later she **p.20** worked as an **editor** of a children's magazine called *Merry's Museum* and as a companion to an invalid friend.

TITLES

Little Women, 1868-1869

An Old-Fashioned Girl, 1870

Little Men, 1871

Eight Cousins, 1875

Rose in Bloom, 1876

Under the Lilacs, 1878

Jack and Jill, 1880

Jo's Boys, and How They Turned Out, 1886

Behind a Mask: The Unknown Thrillers of Louisa May Alcott, 1975

A Double Life: Newly Discovered Thrillers of Louisa May Alcott, 1988

From Jo March's Attic: Stories of Intrigue and Suspense, 1993

Louisa May Alcott Unmasked: Collected Thrillers, 1995

Writing, however, was always Louisa's true vocation. As children, she and her sisters were required to keep journals that their parents read and commented upon, and Bronson Alcott's educational philosophy encouraged his children to read widely and voraciously. About the time that Louisa began teaching, she also began writing thrillers and mystery stories that she published under the name of A. M. Barnard. However, while these stories brought in much-needed money, she also wanted to write "serious" fiction. After a few false starts, she was approached by a publisher looking for novels for girls. Alcott's novel based on her memories of childhood, *Little Women*, established her as a fresh voice in the writing of realistic, rather than sentimental, children's fiction. Her fictional March sisters—Meg, Jo, Beth, and Amy, based on herself and her sisters—were, for their time, remarkably independent, intellectual, and adventurous.

Suffrage Movement

Up until 1920, American women were not allowed to vote. The suffrage movement was the struggle for women to gain the right to vote. The movement began to take shape along side the fight to end slavery. As they struggled to free the slaves, women saw that they also were not being given equal rights. In 1848, the participants in the Seneca Falls Women's Rights Convention drafted a proposal for equal rights patterned after the Declaration of Independence. At the end of the Civil War, the states adopted the Thirteenth Amendment abolishing slavery, the Fourteenth defining civil rights, and the Fifteenth giving the freed slaves the right to vote. However, the suffragists soon realized that gender was not included in the Fifteenth Amendment, and that they still lacked the right to vote. Women would fight on until 1920 before they would see the Nineteenth Amendment ratified stating "The right of citizens of the United States to vote shall not be denied or abridged by the United States or by any state on account of sex."

Little Women, the Movies

Little Women has been brought to the movie screen four times, first in 1919 as a silent film, next in 1933 in its most famous version, again in 1949, and most recently in 1994. It seems that the universal themes of family, love, illness, and difficult times give the story appeal to people in many different eras. For example, in 1933 the country was going through the Great Depression, and many people were out of work or had lost much of their savings. They related to the story of a family holding life together while the father was away at war. In the 1994 version, the director took the opportunity to emphasize feminism, a timely issue that also was embraced by the author during her lifetime.

Alcott continued to write novels following the lives of the Marches and their extended family for almost two more decades, exemplifying the superiority of the life of the mind over materialism, the importance of education for both men and women, and the foolishness of social customs that restricted women's freedom and financial independence. Her characters are warm and human and learn their lessons the hard way, often succumbing to temptation and coming to appreciate the more austere, less glamorous sides of life through their own experience, rather than simply being "good" or "bad" from the start.

Beginning in the 1970's, at a time when Alcott's brand of feminism seemed outdated and scarcely "feminist" at all, interest returned to her thriller and mystery fiction. Several collections of the stories and novels have been published since 1975, allowing readers to see exactly what kind of stories Jo March wrote with such subversive pleasure. *Little Women* has been made into a movie several times, most notably in 1933 with Katharine Hepburn as Jo, and in 1994 with Winona Ryder in the same role.

– Leslie Ellen Jones

Lloyd Alexander

Born: January 30, 1924; Philadelphia, Pennsylvania

www.penguinputnam.com/Author/
AuthorFrame?0000000316

p.437

p.657

p.87

Born in Philadelphia, **Lloyd Alexander** has spent most of his life in that city and its vicinity. When he was five, his father, a **stockbroker**, was bankrupted by the great stock market crash of 1929, and the family had to struggle to keep afloat throughout the ensuing **Great Depression** years. Alexander was a voracious reader and writer as a child and by the age of fifteen had decided that he wanted to be a poet. His parents suggested that he might consider learning some more practical skills as well, since poets were not notorious for being well paid.

Lack of money prevented Alexander from going to college, so in 1943, at the height of World War II, he enlisted in the U.S. Army. After serving as an **interpreter and translator** in France, where he met and married a young woman named Janine Denni, he returned to Philadelphia and commenced a series of jobs in the publishing business, as a cartoonist, an **advertising** copy writer, a layout artist, a trademagazine **editor**, and a translator. In 1955, after years of collecting rejection slips, Alexander began to find success writing autobiographical novels.

In the late 1950's and early 1960's Alexander published with increasing frequency both realistic adult novels and children's **fantasy novels**. The latter drew heavily on his fascination with myth. He was particularly interested in the mythology of **Wales**, which survives in only fragmented form in the tales of the *Mabinogi* and in bardic poetry. He initially tried a simple retelling of these medieval ro-

p.688

p.17

p.20

p.18

mances, but ended up using them as background for his own fantasy realm, Prydain.

The five books of Alexander's "Prydain" series follow the adventures and maturing of Taran the Assistant Pig Keeper, who begins as a callow youth with grandiose ideas of heroism and adventure and who slowly grows into a realization of his role in creating a free and peaceful land. Along the way he is accompanied by a cast of characters including Dallben the wizard (who has raised him), Fflewdur Fflam the bard, Princess Eilonwy, and companions Gurgi and Doli.

Alexander's next series is set in Westmark, a land reminiscent of colonial America and medieval Europe, yet engulfed in a revolution remarkably like that of France in the late eighteenth century. The series follows the ad-

Interpreter and Translator

Interpreters and translators both take words from one language and make them understandable to speakers of another language. An interpreter deals with spoken words, while a translator deals with written words. We often see interpreters at international meetings such as a session of the United Nations. The interpreter listens to a speaker through headphones and translates "simultaneously" by converting what he or she hears in one language into another language and speaking it through a microphone to those listening through their own sets of headphones. A translator, on the other hand, takes a written text and converts it into another written language. This can be done with the assistance of dictionaries and other reference books. It is essential that both the interpreter and translator understand the meaning of the original rather than just the words being spoken or read.

ventures of Theo, a printer's **apprentice** who be- p.246
comes involved with a street girl named Mickle and
a plot to overthrow the tyrannical minister Cabbarus. Mickle turns out to be Augusta, the long-lost
princess of Westmark, and Theo helps her to regain
the throne. Then, when she in turn is overthrown by
the ousted Cabbarus, he helps create a democratic
government for his country.

Alexander's third series follows the adventures
of Vesper Holly, a young girl who travels with her
guardian to exotic locales in the 1870's and encounters mystery and intrigue wherever she finds herself. These novels are set in real places and involve
real events, offering doses of history along with adventure. Alexander's nonseries books are also set in
distant lands and times—India, ancient Greece, p.327
China, Africa—and mix myth, history, and adventure in equal parts.

Lloyd Alexander's books have won him many
literary awards, including a **Newbery Medal** for p.102
The High King, a **Newbery Honor Book** award for
The Black Cauldron, and **American
Book Awards** for *Kestrel* and *Westmark*.

– Leslie Ellen Jones

Wales

Wales is part of Great Britain. It occupies a short peninsula on the western side of the island; three
sides are surrounded by water and the eastern side borders England. Wales has managed to re-
tain its unique cultural identity even though it has been administered by England since the 1500's.
The Welsh people are of Celtic origin and have maintained their language. The country has enjoyed a revival of the Welsh language and is now bilingual, with signs in both English and Welsh.
The BBC even broadcasts in Welsh. There is also a strong cultural tradition of spoken folk tales
passed from generation to generation. *The Mabinogian* is the most famous of the Welsh folk tales,
which was first written down in the 1200's. Music also is central to Welsh life with annual musical
celebrations and competitions held throughout the country.

David Almond

Born: May 15, 1951; Newcastle upon Tyne, England

www.davidalmond.com

David Almond creates mysteries with magical, almost dreamlike, and suspense-filled plots. Then he populates them with male and female **protagonists** who are well drawn, powerful and realistic, the types of characters with whom young people can easily identify. Even his secondary characters are individually realized.

As a child growing up in England, Almond wanted to be a writer, scribbling out stories when he was six or seven years old. He realized part of his dream when he became **editor** of *Panurge*, a fiction magazine. However, after six years during which he found no time to pursue creative writing, he resigned his position and began to write fiction while teaching. Originally a writer of adult fiction, Almond wanted to appeal to an audience whose minds were more imaginative, creative, and fluid. He attained his goal when his first young adult novel, *Skellig*, was published. He credits this award-winning novel with teaching him how to write and what to write about.

At the core of each of Almond's novels is the universal theme of the journey toward self-discovery. Each of his characters takes a physical journey and experiences a psychological, sometimes moral, spiritual maturation. Often, the journey is symbolized through the conflict of light versus dark. Michael, the protagonist of *Skellig*, is beset by financial difficulties and the life-threatening illness of his baby sister, and he and his family move to a dilapidated house. There, in the midst of ruin and darkness,

.233

p.20

TITLES

Skellig, 1998

Kit's Wilderness, 1999

Counting Stars, 2000

Heaven Eyes, 2001

Secret Heart, 2002

The Fire Eaters, 2004

Editor

The editor of a magazine has many responsibilities. Foremost among them is to decide what is printed between the magazine's covers. In the case of a fiction magazine, the editor must work with writers and select which fiction works will appear in a magazine issue. This may involve encouraging the writer to make revisions to his or her work before it is published. The editor must consider how each piece published in the magazine contributes to the collection of pieces in the issue. She or he also works with the magazine staff to assure that the works of fiction are typeset, proofread, and produced as pages that are correct and attractive.

both physical and spiritual, Michael meets Skellig, a half-man, half-angelic creature who appears to be ill. By nurturing Skellig and overcoming his own fear, Michael learns about the fragile nature of life and how the transforming, redemptive power of love can overcome death.

In Almond's second novel, *Kit's Wilderness*, Kit and his mother and father return to Stoneygate, an old English coal-mining town, to care for Kit's recently widowed grandfather. In this setting, Almond creates a hauntingly realistic world in which the dark past and the ghosts of dead miners impinge on the present as Kit is enticed to play a game called Death in an old abandoned mining pit. Kit eventually travels into the eternal darkness of the pit, a journey in which he is confronted with the pervasive darkness in his world. In his battle with the darkness, Kit matures morally and spiritually.

In *Heaven Eyes*, three orphan girls escape from their imprisonment in an orphanage and learn some valuable life lessons on the importance of setting their own course in life and determining their own fate on their journey. In *Secret Heart*, Joe, a young man who is a social outcast dreams of meeting a ti-

p.21

ger. In his search for the tiger, Joe learns to believe in himself with the support of Corinna, a friend who encourages him to follow his dreams. Along the way, he realizes the tiger could be inside of him.

Whether David Almond's novels are set in dilapidated houses or in places scarred by mining pits, their landscapes are intriguingly beautiful places. These ancient-like stories are told in lyrical prose that enhances the story lines. Almond has won a number of writing awards, including Britain's prestigious **Whitbread Children's Book of the Year** for *Skellig*, which was also named a Michael L. Printz Honor Book in the United States. *Kit's Wilderness* also won a **Michael Printz Award**, along with many other awards.

– Sharon K. Wilson

.488

Coal Mining in England

Coal is a mineral deposit that is mined from the earth. England and Wales have rich deposits of coal. For many years, coal was a popular source of fuel for both heating, transportation, and industrial power. Many mines were dug into the earth and miners were sent down to remove the coal deposits and bring them to the surface. Mining towns existed throughout England and Wales and provided support for entire villages. However, the work was dangerous and unhealthy. Many miners died in mine accidents. Others contracted diseases, most frequently lung disease from inhaling the coal dust. In recent years, the demand for coal has declined. It is available at a cheaper cost from other countries, and natural gas is a cleaner and more environmentally friendly fuel. Many of the mines have closed and the number of mining jobs has decreased.

Rudolfo A. Anaya

Born: October 30, 1937; Pastura, New Mexico

www.nea.org/readacross/multi/ranaya.html

Inspired by the regional culture and landscape of New Mexico, **Rudolfo A. Anaya** integrates history, spirituality, and other worldly drama into his fiction. His characters struggle to find themselves and their place in the rich cultural mix of **New Mexico**. p.24

Anaya was born in a little village of New Mexico. One of seven children, he was raised in a devout Spanish-speaking and Roman Catholic home immersed in Spanish, Mexican, and Native American folklore. As a boy, he was close to his grandmother, who like the **folk healer** in *Bless Me, Ultima* used p.678 herbs and spiritual powers to heal. He attended public school in Santa Rosa and Albuquerque and earned bachelor's and master's degrees in English at the University of New Mexico. Later he earned a master's degree in guidance and counseling from the same university.

Bless Me, Ultima, Anaya's best-known work, describes the maturation of Antonio Márez. As Antonio grows up, he observes the marital and generational conflicts of family life and discovers stories that account for life's origin and mysteries. Most importantly, he learns from the conflict between the evil Tenorio Trementina and the good Ultima, the village folk healer, or *curandera*, the respected elderly woman of the community who lives with his p.23 family and becomes his spiritual guide.

Alburquerque, a novel whose title reflects the original spelling of New Mexico's chief city, is a story about reasserting origins. The young *protagonist* p.233 Abrán Gonzalez, disoriented by the discovery of his adoption, faces the challenge of understanding the meaning of the enigmatic advice of the local *curandera*, "*tú eres tú*" (you are who you are). As he searches for his birth father, he finds love, determines his goals, and affirms his values. *Jalamanta*, a story of self-discovery, presents a Christ-like character who has been banished from the city to the desert for thirty years for daring to question the authorities' values of self-serving greed and materialism. This book is a strong expression of allegorical themes that are present in all of Anaya's fiction.

Drawing again on New Mexican stories, ancient beliefs, and contemporary culture, Anaya created Sonny Baca, who is part detective, part spiritual seeker. *Zia Summer*, *Rio Grande Fall*, and *Shaman Winter* are mystery novels in which Baca, guided by his mentors, accesses the spiritual world of his ancestors. In so doing he restrains the forces of evil and strengthens his sense of personal identity and empowerment. *My Land Sings* collects folk tales for young readers. Drawing from tales of indigenous New Mexicans and shaping

Curandera

A *curandera* is a Mexican or Mexican American woman healer who uses herbs, massage, diet, ritual, and prayer to treat illness and mental problems. When the Spanish colonized the New World, they did not allow the natives to continue practicing their own medicine, but the natives did so secretly. Their methods are thought by some to use magic and witchcraft. However, as we have come to accept many alternative forms of medical treatment, the *curandera* has become an accepted practioner of alternative health care in many communities.

New Mexico

New Mexico enjoys a rich culture that is unique among the states. Populated for centuries by American Indians, the territory was explored by the Spanish in the 1500's. In 1609 they established the colony of Santa Fe. The Spanish treated the Indians cruelly, and the two cultures struggled to live side by side in forced peace. When Mexico became independent from Spain in 1821, the American traders and trappers who had been sneaking into the territory were welcome. The opening of the Santa Fe Trail created a trade route that allowed the exchange of goods between merchants in Missouri and those in the territory. This main transportation route was heavily traveled by wagon trains. By 1880, it would be replaced by the railroad. In 1848, at the end of war with Mexico, America had won the territory. As a territory, New Mexico was considered a wild and undesirable place because of the conflicts between the three cultures living there: the American Indians, the Spanish and Mexicans, and the Americans. Following the Civil War, more American settlers flocked to the territory hoping to make their fortunes as farmers and ranchers, but they met conflict with the Indians. Eventually peace was established, the population grew, and in 1912, New Mexico became a state. To this day, New Mexico reflects the three cultures of its inhabitants. It is known as the "land of enchantment" for its rich culture and beautiful landscape.

new stories, Anaya creates new legends with young heroes and heroines of courage and spunk.

A major contemporary Mexican American writer, Rudolfo A. Anaya has inspired a large body of critical study. *Bless Me, Ultima* appears frequently in high school and college curricula. For it, he won the **Premio Quinto Sol** literary award in 1971. He has won grants from the National Endowment for the Arts, the National Chicano Council of Higher Education, and a Kellogg Fellowship.

– Bernadette Flynn Low

Laurie Halse Anderson

Born: October 23, 1961; Potsdam, New York

www.writerlady.com

Writing in a variety of genres for a variety of ages, **Laurie Halse Anderson** is a versatile author with an incisive, humorous style. She enjoys writing both historical novels and contemporary novels, both of which offer unique challenges and rewards. Her first novel, *Speak*, a contemporary story, was a finalist for the **National Book Award** and received several other major awards. The book catapulted Anderson from a relatively unknown author of children's books to a prominent voice in young adult literature who has often been compared with J. D. Salinger and Robert Cormier.

The daughter of a minister and a manager, Anderson has been an avid reader and writer since her childhood. She received a degree in languages and linguistics from **Georgetown University** in 1984 and went on to raise a family while pursuing her writing interests, including a stint as a reporter for the *Philadelphia Inquirer*. She worked at her children's writing for a number of years before getting published and, upon receiving the **Golden Kite Award** for *Speak*, credited the **Society of Children's Book Writers and Illustrators** for providing the community she needed to write novels.

Anderson's idea for the protagonist in *Speak* came to her in a bad dream. Her nightmare, which she wrote down upon waking, became the story of Melinda Sordino, who alienates everyone in her high school by calling the police during a drinking party the summer before her freshman year.

p.117
p.122
p.26
p.111
p.11
p.233

Melinda becomes a silent outcast, a stranger even from herself. In an honest and biting satire of high school culture, Anderson shows the painful healing process that Melinda goes through as she confronts the truth about what happened at the party. She was raped—and to prevent others from experiencing the same victimization, she must speak out.

To accomplish the sharp realism in *Speak* for which she has been often praised, Anderson drew upon her own traumatic memories of tight social cliques in high school. *Catalyst*, with a minister's daughter as its protagonist, also has roots in Anderson's personal experiences. Unlike Anderson, however, its eighteen-year-old protagonist, Kate Malone, feels her life unravel during her senior year, with her rejection from MIT acting as the catalyst.

Fever 1793, named a **Best Book for Young Adults** by the American Library Association, departs from contemporary realism to depict the post-revolutionary yellow fever outbreak in Philadelphia from the viewpoint of sixteen-year-old Matilda Cook.

 p.45

p.480

p.27

Georgetown University

Georgetown University is located in Washington, D.C., and lends its name to a part of the city. It was founded as a Catholic Jesuit university in 1789 by Father John Carroll. It received a federal charter in 1815 and began graduating students with the Bachelor of Arts degree two years later. Father Patrick Healy, president of the university from 1874 to 1882, was influential in the development of the university as a modern research institu-

tion. As the son of an Irish immigrant and a former slave, he was the first African American to earn a Ph.D. and the first to head a predominately white university. This accomplishment was notable at a school that was a "Southern" university prior to the Civil War.

Yellow Fever

Yellow fever is a tropical disease found only in Africa and South America. It is caused by a mosquito-bourne virus that infects the liver, kidneys, and heart muscle. Three to fourteen days after being infected, a patient develops headache, fever, and muscle pain. In serious cases, the patient becomes disoriented, the pulse slows, and the person's skin and whites of the eyes may become yellow from jaundice. Treatment involves bed rest, fluid intake, drugs to reduce the clotting of blood, and blood transfusion. Up to 20 percent of those infected die. In 1900, the Surgeon General of the United States sent a commission, led by army medical scientist Dr. Walter Reed, to Cuba to study an outbreak of yellow fever. After some investigation, the commission established that infection occurred from the bite of the *Aedes aegypti* mosquito. By the end of 1901, the mosquito population had been controlled and yellow fever ceased to be a problem in Cuba. Vaccinations now exist that protect humans from getting the disease.

Some reviewers have criticized *Catalyst* and *Fever* for weaknesses in characterization and plotting. However, all Laurie Halse Anderson's books remain highly popular with young readers, who identify with Anderson's honest portrayal of adolescence. Anderson's humor and rapport with audiences make her a popular speaker on the school visit and conference lecture circuit.

— Lisa Rowe Fraustino

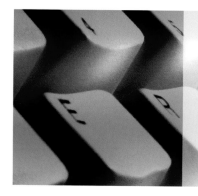

Jennifer Armstrong

Born: May 12, 1961; Waltham, Massachusetts

www.jennifer-armstrong.com

p.117

p.233

p.398

p.30

p.29

Of the dozens of fictional works written by **Jennifer Armstrong** for children and adolescents, her best-known books are her historical novels. These combine careful research with poetic writing, strong characterization, and complex narratives following more than one protagonist.

As a child, Armstrong preferred playing with words to playing with Play-Doh or fingerpaint. After graduating from **Smith College** in 1983, she took a job as an assistant editor with a **packager** of juvenile series books. In the process of working on some of the best-known series in young adult publishing, she decided to give writing a try. She began by writing books for the popular "Sweet Valley High" series. Before long she was writing for the packager full time. Eventually she branched out on her own with *Steal Away*, a story of interracial understanding that met with immediate success, becoming a Young Adult Library Services Association **Popular Paperback for Young Adults**. She went on to propose new series ideas to be published under her own name. She also wrote series titles under the pseudonym of Julia Winfield.

With a narrative switching back and forth in time between the 1850's and the 1890's, *Steal Away* explores the friendship of two thirteen-year-olds during the era of slavery. Susannah, born in the North, is given her own personal slave when she is orphaned and goes to live with her uncle in Virginia. She does not believe in slavery, however, and treats her personal slave, Bethlehem, as a friend. She even secretly teaches Bethlehem how to read. Eventually, the two girls steal themselves away to the North with the help of the **Underground Railroad**. Forty years later they reunite to tell their story to the next generation.

In *The Dreams of Mairhe Mehan*, Armstrong again uses an intertwined narrative style to tell the story of an Irish immigrant family. Mary, the protagonist, works as a maid in a tavern during the Civil War, in which her brother is fighting for the Union forces. Mary becomes a nurse in a sequel, *Mary Mehan Awake*, and falls in love with a hired hand who has lost his hearing in the war. Of all her books, Armstrong is proudest of these two, which she calls "the most calculated, the most intricately planned and designed."

Armstrong's immigrant theme continues in the Wild Rose Inn series of six books about six generations of Mackenzie women, beginning with Birdie, a Scottish girl who settles in the Massachusetts Bay

Sweet Valley High Series

The Sweet Valley High series of books was created by Francine Pascal. Its main characters are twins, Jessica and Elizabeth Wakefield, who live in a Southern California town. The series originally was meant to be a television series, but Pascal created books instead. The stories in the series concern typical problems encountered by school age kids. The popularity of the series resulted in more and more books in addition to the television series.

Colony. The Fire-Us trilogy, which Armstrong wrote with Nancy Butcher, jumps ahead to the future in a series of science-fiction stories about a band of young people who seem to be the only survivors of a catastrophic virus.

Steal Away remains Jennifer Armstrong's most honored work of fiction as an American Library Association Best Book for Young Adults and a Golden Kite Honor Book for the Society of Children's Book Writers and Illustrators. Her most widely taught and acclaimed book, however, is *Shipwreck at the Bottom of the World* (1998), a work of nonfiction about Ernest Shackleton's Antarctic expedition. She has also edited original anthologies of short fiction for young adults that have been well received.

p.45

p.111

p.480

p.11

– Lisa Rowe Fraustino

Book Packager

A book packager is a company that creates books for a publisher. It can consist of a fully organized business or a loosely organized group of editors, proofreaders, designers, and production editors. The publishers, who do not have enough employees to create or produce all of the books they publish, come to the packager with an idea for a book. It may be a topic, an outline, or a completed manuscript. The packager is paid a fee to develop the idea or manuscript into a file that can be sent to the printer. The packager will create and edit the text, acquire photos or illustrations to accompany the text, lay out the text and illustrations into attractive pages, and create a digital file that can be sent to the printer. The printer will then produce the books. The publisher is responsible for advertising the book, distributing it to bookstores, and selling copies of the book.

Jane Austen

Born: December 16, 1775; Steventon, England
Died: July 18, 1817; Winchester, England
www.austen.com/onaust.htm

Jane Austen's novels remain popular because her writing style is concise, flexible, and animated and yet unadorned. Her dialogue, without resort to slang, shows a precise ear for individual and revealing rhythms of speech. Her ironic detachment and technical skill have established her reputation with modern critics, but the deftness with which she pleases and instructs has endeared her works to generations of readers, young and old.

Austen lived a quiet life as the daughter of an Anglican priest and sister of six ambitious brothers and one sister. Her sister, Cassandra, two years her elder, was her closest friend and confidante. Austen never married, although she had three suitors. One was a charming Irish man who had prospects but no fortune, and therefore the romance was broken off through the intervention of their families. One was a clergyman who offered the prospect of a quiet, secure life, but he died before he had a chance to make a proposal. The third was a gauche but wealthy man six years Austen's junior whom she accepted in a moment of pure financial practicality; however, she changed her mind the next day, much to everyone's embarrassment. All three types of male suitors appear in Austen's novels. After her father's death, Jane, Cassandra, and their mother were dependent upon the generosity of other members of the family, especially her brothers, for financial support. While that support was given freely, the Austen women were acutely aware of the re-

TITLES

Sense and Sensibility, 1811

Pride and Prejudice, 1813

Mansfield Park, 1814

Emma, 1815

Northanger Abbey, 1818

Persuasion, 1818

Sanditon, 1871

Love and Friendship and Other Early Works, 1922

English Class System

English society was divided into the upper class and the lower class. The upper class owned property; the lower class worked for the upper class as farm help or as household help but did not own anything. As cities grew and commercial activity developed in services and manufacturing, the middle class emerged. This class was populated largely by those members of the upper class who failed to inherit the wealth of their ancestors. A practice call primogeniture gave the eldest son of a family the exclusive right of inheritance. This often left younger brothers and sisters with a small inheritance at best, not enough to live in the way they had while growing up in their parent's home. They often entered the fields of education, clergy, or the military. For many, marriage was a way to secure a comfortable economic future. A daughter of a wealthy family would attempt to marry well since she would not inherit from her family.

strictions that lack of a personal fortune forced upon women in the early nineteenth century.

Austen wrote novels depicting the world she knew and the life she led. Her plots revolve around women's problems in finding suitable husbands, the conflicts between romantic love and intellectual compatibility on the one hand and practical, financial concerns and social status on the other. She sets scenes in country houses and small villages, occasionally in the English resort spa of Bath, and only rarely in the more glamorous capital of London. Her characters are members of the gentry, often with family connections to the nobility, as the Austens themselves had, but generally lacking abundant income. Their lives revolve around social visits, dances, housekeeping, and gossip. Formal education, especially for women, is not of particular interest, but reading is; the best indicator of romantic compatibility in an Austen novel is shared literary tastes.

Perhaps the classic Austen novel is her second, *Pride and Prejudice*, in which the five Bennet sisters, Jane, Elizabeth, Mary, Kitty, and Lydia attempt to find themselves suitable and compatible husbands. Elizabeth triumphs over antagonistic aristocrats, her sister Lydia's scandalous elopement, and her own unexamined assumptions to marry the wealthy Mr. Darcy. Similarly, in *Emma*, the heroine comes to realize that her assessments of what is best for others can be seriously misguided. Anne Elliot, the heroine of *Persuasion*, learns that she must rely on her own judgment of what will make her happy rather than succumbing to the pressures of her family and friends.

Austen preferred to live a quiet, anonymous country life and shrank from celebrity. Nonetheless, her acquaintance with the wider world increased both through her status as a published writer and through her brothers' social and career successes. Her later novels, particularly *Persuasion* and the unfinished *Sanditon*, exhibited a growing awareness of the outside world and the expanding British Empire, yet still reflected life through women's experience and interests.

p.33 All of Jane Austen's novels have been turned into movies and television miniseries. Emma Thompson won an Oscar for her adaptation of *Sense and Sensibility* (1995). In addition to direct screen adaptations, *Emma* was updated to 1990's Beverly Hills, California, in *Clueless* (1995).

— Leslie Ellen Jones

Novels into Film

Austen's novels have become popular as film adaptations. In 1995 alone, two popular films appeared based on Austen novels. *Clueless* was a popular Hollywood comedy based on Austen's *Emma* but presented as a contemporary story set at Beverly Hills High School. It later appeared as a weekly television series. It was followed by the academy award-winning British film *Sense and Sensibility*. That both films were popular at the box office reveals our interest in Austen's novels of manners. Much like popular soap operas, Austen's stories reveal the motives, emotions, misunderstandings, and resolutions to relationships and marriages. They include class differences, money, love, and practicality as issues that influence behavior. As the films show us, human nature was the same in the early 19th century as it is today.

Avi

Born: December 23, 1937; New York, New York

www.avi-writer.com

Avi (pronounced ah-vee) Wortis publishes under his first name only. Among the most prolific and most honored young adult novelists currently writing, he is a master of creating stories that present crucial situations realistically. His use of language is visual and effective. His young protagonists always maintain their integrity in sharp contrast to the adults with whom they deal. p.233

The son of a psychiatrist and a social worker, Avi holds degrees from the University of Wisconsin and Columbia University and has had a long career as a librarian in the New York City Public Library System and at Trenton State College in New Jersey. p.35 He first became interested in writing fiction when his sons urged him to concoct stories for them as they were growing up. Avi has compared himself to a dentist: Just as a dentist sees teeth everywhere, he sees story ideas everywhere.

Avi's fiftieth young adult novel, the action-packed *Crispin: The Cross of Lead*, recipient of both p.102 **Newbery** and **Caldecott Medals**, is the gripping story of a thirteen-year-old boy in fourteenth century England. The illegitimate son of the lord of the manor, Crispin grows up not knowing his true name. When his mother dies, Aycliffe, steward of the manor, declares Crispin a "wolf's head," meaning that

Librarian

We know the librarian as a person who works in the library helping us find books to read and locate information needed to write reports. But the training and job of the librarian is much more complicated than what we see. Most librarians attend a university that grants a Masters degree in library or information science. There are many technical skills that the librarian learns in preparation for a job in the library. Now that computers play such a large role in how we access information, librarians must learn about both how computers work, how to establish a computer network, and also how to search the Internet and specialized databases to retrieve authoritative information on a wide variety of subjects. In addition, librarians learn how to select books for the library that will meet the interests of library patrons and how to use professional systems to categorize those books so they can be easily located in the library. They learn management skills that help keep the library operating as an efficient business, by serving patrons in the library or through remote access at home, and by circulating books and making sure they are returned to the shelves. They also must work with budgets to keep the library operating with the money made available and raise funds to help with programs their budget cannot support. Librarians are important people in both our schools and our communities.

anyone can kill him without fear of retribution. Carrying with him only his mother's lead cross, given to him by a priest who tells him his real name and who is subsequently murdered, Crispin flees. He meets Bear, a wandering juggler, who becomes his protector. The bond between the two is particularly touching. It is ultimately revealed that Crispin is Aspa's son and heir, but Crispin shuns his inheritance out of loyalty to Bear.

The True Confessions of Charlotte Doyle is another thriller in which thirteen-year-old Charlotte Doyle embarks on a transatlantic voyage by herself in 1832. She is secretly given a knife by the ship's cook. When a murder occurs on board, Charlotte is the main suspect and is tried for the crime. This truly compelling book received Golden Kite and Boston Globe-Horn Book Awards and was named a **Newbery Honor Book**.

p.111

p.747

In *Nothing but the Truth*, Philip Malory, a ninth grade student, causes a disturbance in his school by humming during the national anthem. The story, documented by a combination of letters, reports, diaries, and memos, presents a milder image of public high schools in the 1990's than is usually projected. This novel was also named a **Newbery Honor Book** and a **Boston Globe-Horn Honor Book**.

Avi is often concerned with the coming-of-age problems of young boys. In *Don't You Know There's a p.36 War On?*, set in **Brooklyn**, New York, during World War II, a sixteen-year-old protagonist copes with a variety of personal problems, including failing math grades, alarming air raid drills, a crush on one of his teachers, and a deep concern that his father, a merchant marine who sails across the dangerous North Atlantic, will not survive the war.

Avi's other writing honors include the **Christopher Award** for *Encounter at Easton*, the Scott p.51 O'Dell Award for Historical Fiction for *The Fighting Ground*, and a **Boston Globe-Horn Book Award** for *Poppy*.

– R. Baird Shuman

Brooklyn Bridge

In 1860, Brooklyn was the third largest city in the U.S., but it was still separated from Manhattan by the East River. By 1867, plans were made to build a suspension bridge joining the two cities. This marvel of engineering was completed in 1883, allowing travel and trade to occur more easily. Greater New York City was created in 1898, bringing together the cities of Manhattan, Brooklyn, Queens, the Bronx, and Staten Island. Today, the Brooklyn Bridge remains one our national treasures and is crossed by more than 150,000 vehicles a day.

Natalie Babbitt

Born: July 28, 1932; Dayton, Ohio

www.kidsreads.com/authors/au-babbitt-natalie.asp

Natalie Babbitt's work shows her versatility in exploring both realistic problems and philosophical issues such as immortality, particularly in her best-known novel, *Tuck Everlasting*. Babbitt credits her young characters with the ability to deal with both difficult and sometimes abstract issues and the more mundane problems of everyday life. She is a master at developing vivid images that recreate a world of sound, picture, smell, and touch. Readers of her books explore ideas, personalities, and fascinating stories in rich detail.

Born in Ohio, Babbitt married Samuel Fisher Babbitt in 1954 and had three children. Her background in art at both the Cleveland School of Art and Smith College led her into book illustration for a p.398 time early in her career and then again later in a series of books of poetry by Valerie Worth. However, p.38 she is best known for her writing both for children and for young adults.

Tuck Everlasting is an ambitious story about ten-year-old Winnie Foster's dilemma of whether to drink from the spring of immortality and live forever or to spurn the water and live a normal life. She is tempted by the idea of eternal life with the attractive seventeen-year-old Jesse but carefully ponders the ramifications of this choice. What happens when the wheel of life stops turning and people no longer need to cope with the specter of death? Babbitt's story forces young readers to consider the rather abstract and philosophic notion of what it means to die, but she broaches it through vivid characterization

TITLES

Phoebe's Revolt, 1968

The Search for Delicious, 1969

Kneeknock Rise, 1970

Goody Hall, 1971

The Devil's Storybook, 1974

Tuck Everlasting, 1975

The Eyes of the Amaryllis, 1977

The Devil's Other Storybook, 1987

and the real-life suspense of Winnie's meeting with the Tucks.

The Eyes of the Amaryllis recounts the story of a tragic accident at sea and how a young girl begins to understand the feelings and actions of her grandmother, who searches the sea for the lost ship that claimed her husband's life. Once again, Babbitt surrounds a basically philosophical theme with vivid images and the compelling stories of real people in a real family.

One of Babbitt's earlier novels, *The Search for Delicious*, follows the quest of twelve-year-old Gaylen as he scours the kingdom for the meaning of the word "delicious." In this mythic **fantasy**, the boy matures through his adventures to face the ultimate challenge of saving the kingdom.

p.87

Natalie Babbitt has embraced challenging and serious topics in her work for younger readers and has made these ideas immediate, vivid, and readily accessible in a versatile range of novels. Her novels exhibit an unusual and fascinating blend of fantasy and reality. Her

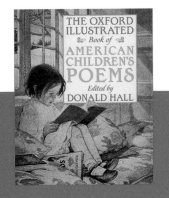

Illustrator

An illustrator draws pictures for a book, poster, or advertisement. The illustrator of a book also may be the author or may work with an author. Most book illustrators work on books for children. Illustrators develop a distinctive style, and readers will come to recognize the work of well-known illustrators. The collaboration between a children's book author and illustrator is so important they are both represented by the same professional association: The Society of Children's Book Writers and Illustrators.

Tuck Everlasting, the Movie

The film version of *Tuck Everlasting* was released by Disney in 2002. When books are made into films, there are usually some changes in the story. In this adaptation, the major change is that Winnie is now seventeen years old instead of ten. That means her reaction to Jesse, the seventeen-year-old Tuck son, is much more romantic than in the book. Jesse, of course, has a different reaction to a girl his own age than he does to a ten year old. Also, Miles is a deeper character in the movie, and his path to immortality has a darker impact on his character. Reading the book and seeing the movie will spark conversation about the similarities and differences, as well as further thoughts on what it means to live and die.

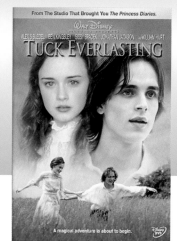

work has received numerous honors. *Tuck Everlasting* won many awards, including the prestigious **Christopher Award**. *Kneeknock Rise* was recognized as a **Newbery Honor Book**, and *The Devil's Storybook* was a **National Book Award** finalist. Both *The Eyes of the Amaryllis* and *Tuck Everlasting* have been made into **feature-length films**.

– Ann M. Cameron

.102

p.122

.39

Kitty Barne

Born: 1883; England
Died: 1957; England

Kitty Barne wrote mostly children's fiction but is best known as the author of *Visitors from London*. This award-winning novel about London children transported to a country village during World War II is often regarded as the first realistic story for young readers about life in wartime England.

As a child growing up in rural England, Marion Catherine Barne, nicknamed Kitty, had two major interests: drama and music. In elementary school, she produced a play and started a dramatic society. At eleven, she began playing in an orchestra. She completed her education at the Royal College of Music in London. Although she had a lifelong interest in music, she eventually decided to be a playwright. However, none of the eighteen plays she wrote between 1910 and 1947 achieved any notable success.

Kitty Barne married Eric Streatfeild and knew his cousin Noel Streatfeild, a popular children's writer. It was probably at his suggestion that she tried her hand at writing children's fiction. The result was a mystery, *The Easter Holidays* (1935; later republished as *Secret of the Sandhills*, 1949). Three years later, with the appearance of *She Shall Have Music* (1938), the story of an aspiring young musician, Barne's reputation as a children's writer was established.

The following year, Barne wrote another novel based on her own experience. In *Family Footlights*, the four Farrar children find themselves spending their Christmas holidays in Sussex with their aunt Myra, and decide to put on a play. As others in the community become involved, new talents are discovered and lasting friendships are made. Reviewers of this book noted how realistically Barne described the characters' pettiness, jealousy, and fits of temperament, as well as the maddening mixups in the production, that only made the final success of the venture more satisfying.

This approach is also evident in *Visitors from London*. Again the Farrar children are visiting Sussex. However, now World War II has broken out, and their aunt Myra has been assigned to turn an old house into a refuge for thirty-five children who have p.59 been **evacuated** from London because of **German bombing raids** on the capital city. p.41 There are many problems, some of them very funny: the attempts of the Farrars to improvise when supplies do not arrive, for example, and their efforts at dealing with children who have never seen barnyard animals. However, Barne does not underplay the evacuees' emotional stress. Some of the city children never adapt to rural life. However, a few come to love coun-

Battle of Britain

The Battle of Britain, fought in the air, was the first major defeat of German armed forces in World War II. In 1940, Germany had conquered the countries of Belgium, Holland, and France. The British knew that they would be Adolf Hitler's next target. With the Royal Navy protecting the Atlantic supply routes provided by the U.S., the defense of Great Britain was left to the Royal Air Force. In July and August, 1940, the Germans launched Operation Sea Lion, bombing ships in the English Channel, the port city of Dover, and military sites in southeastern England. They next moved the bombing to other ports and airfields, and in September the bombing was shifted to London. After attacks on September 7 and 9, the final battle came on September 15. In an air battle that lasted from noon until the evening, sixty Nazi planes were destroyed, while the British lost only twenty-six aircraft. Hitler abandoned Operation Sea Lion and turned his attention to the invasion of the Soviet Union.

The Carnegie Medal

The Carnegie Medal was established in 1936 in memory of Andrew Carnegie. Carnegie was born in Scotland in 1835. He immigrated to the United States where he made a fortune in the steel industry. His boyhood experience in the library inspired him to set up more than 2,800 libraries in the English-speaking world. The Carnegie Medal honors an outstanding book written for children or young adults in English and published in the United Kingdom. It is awarded by the Chartered Institute of Librarians and Information Professionals (CILIP) in July at Under the Covers, a conference on childrens books and libraries. The winner receives a golden medal and £500 worth of books donated to a library of the winner's choice.

try life, and most of the Londoners display the kind of matter-of-fact courage that enabled the British people to survive the horrors of the war.

Kitty Barne is recognized as one of the first writers to believe that young people deserved realistic fiction, rather than escapism. In 1940, *Visitors from London* won the **Carnegie Medal** from the Library Association of the United Kingdom. Although Barne continued to publish children's fiction until shortly before her death in 1957, she is remembered primarily for *Visitors from London*, which is still considered one of the finest books for young people produced during World War II.

– Rosemary M. Canfield Reisman

p.42

Tracy Barrett

Born: March 1, 1955; Cleveland, Ohio

www.tracybarrett.com

Tracy Barrett's historical novel *Anna of Byzantium* makes the Middle Ages seem as real as early America does in her many works of nonfiction. Although the setting of the book may be unfamiliar to most modern-day readers, the family conflicts are not. Young women, in particular, can understand the feelings of the title character when, after being trained to rule a great empire, she is shunted aside as soon as a male heir to the throne is born.

Barrett was born in Cleveland, Ohio, the daughter of a psychologist and a teacher. As a child, she dreamed of becoming a writer, but she later trained for an academic career. She graduated from Brown University in 1976 with a major in classics, joined the faculty of Vanderbilt University as a lecturer in Italian in 1984, and in 1988 earned a doctorate in Italian and French from the University of California at Berkeley. Meanwhile, she married Gregory Giles, with whom she had two children.

While Barrett was still an undergraduate, she wrote five children's stories for an educational series. However, she did not return to nonacademic writing until 1992. Feeling that she needed a change from teaching, translating, and writing scholarly articles, she de-

TITLE

Anna of Byzantium, 1999

Byzantium

Ancient Byzantium was a Greek city and seaport chosen to become the capital of the new Eastern Roman Empire in 330 C.E. by Roman emperor Constantine the Great. He expanded the city and re-named it Constantinople. Located on the Bosphorus, the strait separating Europe from Asia, Constantinople became the largest and most significant city in Europe. Constantinople was re-named Istanbul in 1930, and is part of the republic of Turkey.

cided to use her research skills to produce books for young readers that focused on great events in American history. The results included *Nat Turner and the Slave Revolt* (1993) and *Harpers Ferry: The Story of John Brown's Raid* (1994). Those works were followed by *Growing Up in Colonial America* (1995) and three books about southern states.

Anna of Byzantium was Barrett's first venture into long fiction. However, like her other books, the novel demanded extensive research. Barrett had become interested in the life of Anna Comnena, a twelfth century Greek princess who became one of the most important writers of her time. This book focuses on the events that brought Anna, at seventeen, to confinement in a convent. Telling Anna's story in the first person, the novel recalls her early life at court, when as the first-born child and presumptive heir of the emperor of **Byzantium**, she is given the kind of education usually reserved for princes, only to be shunted aside when her mother finally gives birth to a boy. No longer the center of attention either at court or in her immediate family, Anna broods until, encouraged by her manipulative grandmother, she resolves to have her brother killed. When the plot fails, Anna is sent to live in a convent. However, her life is not over. At the end of the novel, she is shown as having come to see that her downfall was the result of her own vanity and pride. As a reward for her new humility, she finds her true vocation as a scholar and writer.

Tracy Barrett once stated that her goal in writing for children and young adults was to create narratives that made complex events comprehensible. In her first work of fiction, she has again accomplished that difficult task. *Anna of Byzantium* was named a **Best Book for Young Adults** by the **American Library Association**.

p.480

– Rosemary M. Canfield Reisman

American Library Association

With more than 64,000 members, the American Library Association (ALA) is a professional organization that represents the interests of libraries and librarians. Its headquarters are located in Chicago, Illinois and it maintains an office in Washington, D.C. Libraries, businesses, and individuals can become members by paying annual dues. The ALA publishes a number of journals with articles and book reviews of interest to library professionals. The organization also sponsers educational conferences for librarians. ALA works to promote decent working conditions and wages for library personnel, and lobbies the government to secure funds for library programs, to protect First Amendment rights, and to guarantee equal access of information for all Americans.

T. A. Barron

Born: March 26, 1952; Boston, Massachusetts

www.tabarron.com

Thomas Archibald Barron's novels feature heroic youngsters who face agonizing decisions. They have high ideals and hopes, but also basic human weaknesses that can put themselves and their friends into great danger. He writes action-packed stories with wonderful characters.

Born in Boston, Barron grew up in both New England and Colorado and always loved the wilderness. He was a bright student and attended Princeton University, **Oxford University** (as a **Rhodes Scholar**), and Harvard University. After finishing his education, he made a great deal of money at a New York venture-capital firm, but what he really wanted to do was write. He was lucky when the popular author Madeleine L'Engle agreed to look at his first **manuscript**. She gave it to her agent, who sold it to a publisher. Barron then surprised his business colleagues when he quit the firm, returned to Colorado with his wife and five children, and began writing full time.

Barron's first novel, *Heartlight*, introduces spunky Kate, whose grandfather invents a means of traveling faster than the speed of light. They then embark on a race-against-time mission to save the Sun from a premature death and encounter amazing creatures on the planet Trethoniel. Barron's second book was *The Ancient One*. While visiting her great-aunt Melanie, twelve-year-old Kate finds that the Oregon loggers have learned about a secret, ancient redwood forest hidden in the crater of a dead volcano. The men in the nearby town then begin to cut down

p.173

p.47

p.62

the trees illegally. Meanwhile, Kate and a delinquent boy named Jody go back five centuries through a time tunnel and face the monster Gashra, who is bent on destroying the same forest. Even stronger magic and greater suspense fill *The Merlin Effect*, in which Kate, now thirteen, joins her father and two scientists investigating a strange whirlpool and a sunken treasure ship off the coast of Baja California. After learning about the magical ancient Horn of Merlin, Kate is lost on an island trapped by a mystical whirlpool and is drawn into a centuries-old conflict between Merlin and the evil **sorceress** Nimue.

While researching for *The Merlin Effect*, Barron became fascinated with **Arthurian lore**. Readers who enjoy Susan Cooper's Dark Is Rising series and Lloyd Alexander's Prydain Chronicles are certain to enjoy *The Lost Years of Merlin*. In that story, a young boy with no memory of his past washes ashore on the coast of **Wales**. He discovers he has magical powers and learns he is the

Rhodes Scholarship

The prestigious Rhodes Scholarship program was founded in 1902 after the death of Cecil John Rhodes, an English statesman made wealthy from profits achieved through the founding of Rhodesia (now, Zimbabwe) in Africa. It brings outstanding students from many countries to Oxford University in England. American students have been participating in the program since 1904. Each year thirty-two American students are selected from the hundreds of college and university applicants. The successful applicant not only has a solid undergraduate education but also demonstrates evidence of broader interests and achievements. Scholars receive all tuition, fees, living and travel expenses for two years of study, with a possible third year extension.

Arthurian Lore

The legend of King Arthur appears in many works of literature. One of the best known is *Le Morte d'Arthur*, by Sir Thomas Malory. First printed in 1485, this version of the King Arthur story borrowed from previous sources, moving the location of the story to England. It also gave new order to the events, providing more of a story. The legend has appeared on the stage and in film as the musical *Camelot*, in an animated Disney film *The Sword in the Stone*, and in numerous books from Tennyson's poem *Idylls of the King* to Twain's *A Connecticut Yankee in King Arthur's Court*. The familiar characters are King Arthur, Queen Guinevere, Merlin the magician, Sir Lancelot, Galahad, Tristram and Isolde, Sir Mordred, and the Lady of the Lake. The familiar setting is Camelot.

young wizard Merlin, who will grow up to be mentor of England's King Arthur. He journeys to the magical island of Fincayra and survives a series of fantastic adventures. In *The Seven Songs of Merlin*, he must interpret seven prophecies that will give him greater powers. Merlin makes mistakes because of his pride and awkwardness but gradually comes to trust other people and helps save the world.

In *The Fires of Merlin*, Merlin faces fire in many different forms and loses his magical powers. The boy (and future king) Arthur makes his first appearance in *The Mirror of Merlin*, and their adventures lead them and a wonderful deer-girl to encounter a haunted marsh, talking trees, dragons, and a creature called the ballymag. In *The Wings of Merlin*, Fincayra is threatened by a warrior with swords for arms and by the evil sorcerer Stangmar. In all these exciting books, Merlin moves toward his ultimate destiny.

In 1997 the American Library Association named *The Lost Years of Merlin* one of the year's Best Books for Young Adults.

p.4

p.480

– Fiona Kelleghan

Miriam Bat-Ami
Born: June 26, 1950; Scranton, Pennsylvania

Miriam Bat-Ami is a scholar as well as a creative writer who specializes in children's and adolescent literature. Most of her published works have been picture books and middle-grade novels. Religious themes often predominate in her work, as in her most renowned novel for young adults, *Two Suns in the Sky*, a love story involving a Roman Catholic American girl and a Jewish Croatian who meet in a refugee camp in New York during the **Holocaust**.

The daughter of a violinist and a rabbi, Bat-Ami was born in Pennsylvania and grew up with a flair for speech and a desire to move audiences to laughter and tears. As a teenager she wanted to dance with a **ballet** company. She attended Hebrew University in Jerusalem, and upon her return to the United States, she felt that she had roots in both countries. This feeling would many years later shape her novel *Two Suns in the Sky*. After graduating from college, she spent several years working at various jobs, traveling, and writing. At the age of twenty-eight she went back to school, completed a doctorate at the University of Pittsburgh, and eventually settled in Michigan, where she continues to teach in the English department of Western Michigan University in Kalamazoo. She is married and has two sons who have inspired her writing; in fact, she says that the ages of her **protagonists** and audiences have corresponded with the ages of her sons growing up.

During World War II, the United States established a refugee shelter for European Jews at Fort

TITLE

Two Suns in the Sky, 1999

p.50

p.722

p.233

The Holocaust

Once dictator Adolf Hitler gained power in Germany in 1933, his Nazi Party began its program of boycotting Jewish-owned businesses and creating laws to take away civil rights from Jewish people. The harassment led to an official policy of destroying all Jews. Concentration camps were built and Jewish men, women, and children were transported to them by train. Stripped of all personal belongings and forced to live and work in unbearable conditions, many Jews died as a result of illness or starvation. Many more were tortured, shot to death or killed in large gas chambers. By the end of World War II in 1945, the Nazis had exterminated more than six million Jewish people.

Ontario near Oswego, New York. *Two Suns in the Sky*, a Romeo-and-Juliet story about a forbidden romance, takes place in this setting. When teenagers from the camp attend the area high school, local girl Chris Cook meets refugee Adam Bornstein. Their romance sparks a conflict in her family that is reflected in the community at large. Both the local residents and the camp refugees must learn to live with each other in the changing world. Bat-Ami based many of the characters and themes on actual people and events found in field research, including interviews of Oswego residents.

Miriam Bat-Ami has said of her books that they speak of "family and community, of being inside a group and of feeling left out or outside, of wanting to become part of larger circle." Praised for its thorough research, her *Two Suns in the Sky* received the Scott O'Dell Award for Historical Fiction. It was also named a **Best Book for Young Adults** by the **American Library Association**.

.51

p.45

p.480

– Lisa Rowe Fraustino

The Scott O'Dell Award for Historical Fiction

In 1982, award-winning children's author, Scott O'Dell, established The Scott O'Dell Award for Historical Fiction, with $5,000 going to the author of the selected book. His purpose in establishing the annual award was to encourage writers to create books of historical fiction that would give young readers an appreciation of the past and how it has shaped their country and their world. The winning book must be written for children or young adults, take place in the U.S., Canada, Central America, or South America, be written in English by an American citizen, and have been published by a U.S. publisher. Scott O'Dell was perhaps most famous for his 1962 novel, *Island of the Blue Dolphins*—itself a Newbery Award winner.

Joan Bauer

Born: July 12, 1951; River Forest, Illinois

www.joanbauer.com/jbhome.html

TITLES

The heroines of **Joan Bauer**'s novels have determination, and an independent spirit coupled with a sense of humor. Though her books deal with serious issues, such as paternal neglect and civic corruption, their first-person narrators tell their stories in such a lively manner that the effects are often comic and always positive.

During Bauer's childhood, she and her three sisters delighted in the stories told by their grandmother, who lived with them. From her grandmother, Bauer learned to value humor as a way to survive life's difficulties. It would be a long time before Bauer became a writer. She first spent a decade in advertising, married Evan, a **computer engineer**, and had a daughter, Jean, who was a teenager by the time Bauer was fully established. Bauer credits Jean and her friends for keeping her up-to-date on the issues teenagers face. However, Bauer's attitude toward life again comes directly from her grandmother.

p.705

Bauer's first book, *Squashed*, is the story of an overweight teenager, Ellie Morgan, who is determined to win a pumpkin-growing contest, thus proving her worth to her town, to her father, and, most of all, to herself. Ellie's account of her adventures with her massive pumpkin, Max, is

Mothers Against Drunk Drivers

In 1979, Cindi Lamb's car was hit head-on in Maryland by a drunk driver. The crash left her baby daughter, Laura, without the use of her arms or legs. One year later, Candy Lightner's thirteen-year-old daughter was killed by a drunk driver in California. Candy met with other mothers in Sacramento and founded Mothers Against Drunk Drivers (MADD), a group to support victims and to work to stop drunk driving. Soon Cindi Lamb joined the effort and before long MADD chapters were being formed across the country. Today there are more than 3 million supporters of MADD, and the number of alcohol-related traffic deaths has dropped by 43%. The mission of MADD is "to stop drunk driving, support victims of this violent crime, and prevent underage drinking." MADD holds vigils and poignant demonstrations to highlight their cause.

hilarious. However, the book has a serious side, and Ellie's persistence establishes her as a worthy role model for other young adults.

In *Thwonk*, Bauer again uses humor to make an important point: that it is foolish to fall in love with someone solely because he is good-looking and popular. It is significant that each of Bauer's first two novels ends with its heroine's winning the approval of an indifferent father. The theme of flawed father-daughter relationships is based on Bauer's own experience, since her own father was an **alcoholic** and a compulsive gambler, who deserted his family and finally committed suicide. Bauer has commented that his life demonstrated the importance of the choices one makes.

This emphasis on making choices dominates Bauer's third young adult novel, *Rules of the Road*. In it, the sixteen-year-old narrator, Jenna Boller, chooses to remain loyal to her employer throughout a corporate takeover attempt, thus helping to save

Delacorte Press Prize for a First Young Adult Novel

Delacorte Press Books for Young Readers, a division of Random House, sponsors an annual prize to encourage writers of young adult fiction. U.S. and Canadian authors who have not previosly published a young adult novel are invited to submit book-length manuscripts with contemporary settings suitable for readers between ages 12 and 18. The editors of the press select the winning manuscript. The author wins $1,500 in cash, a $7,500 advance against royalties paid on the sales of the book, and publication by Delacorte Press Books for Young Readers.

the business. Then, after a friend is killed by a **drunk driver**, Jenna makes another difficult decision: She informs the police that her alcoholic father habitually drives drunk. The themes of difficult choices, personal integrity, and parent-child relationships are also central in *Backwater* and *Hope Was Here*. In both novels, sixteen-year-old girls courageously make their way through difficulties and finally learn what it means to be part of a family.

Joan Bauer is consistently praised as a unique writer, whose strong, decent, and funny heroines provide positive role models for her many enthusiastic readers. Among the writing awards that she has won are the **Delacorte Prize for First Young Adult Novel** for *Squashed*; the **Golden Kite Award** for *Rules of the Road*, which was also selected one of the American Library Association's **Best Books for Young Adults**; and a **Newbery Honor Book** award from the **American Library Association** for *Hope Was Here*.

– Rosemary M. Canfield Reisman

p.5

p.5

p.48

p.4

p.111

p.102

Marion Dane Bauer

Born: November 20, 1938; Oglesby, Illinois

www.mariondanebauer.com

Marion Dane Bauer has peopled her novels with characters who face great difficulties in their lives. In *Rain of Fire*, for example, Steve finds himself telling lies, both to make himself look cool to other boys, and to protect his own notions about his older brother, a war veteran and **pacifist**. *On My Honor*'s Joel first tries to deny, and then must confront and learn to live with, the fatal consequences of a lapse in judgement.

Bauer was born in Illinois. Her father, a chemist, was employed in a cement factory much of his working life, and her mother was a teacher. During her early childhood, Bauer lived in a house on the edge of their town, and thus spent hours learning how to entertain herself. She transferred to a school in Peru, Illinois, when she was twelve, and remembers the transition as a difficult one. It is not a coincidence that many of the **protagonists** of her novels are also twelve years old. Bauer has said that part of the energy in her stories comes from the fact that she still finds it necessary to revisit that period in her own life.

Although Bauer wanted to become a writer, she studied language arts in college with the goal of becoming an English teacher. After she married Ron Bauer in 1959, her job as a

.56

233

TITLES

Rain of Fire, 1983

On My Honor, 1986

A Taste of Smoke, 1993

Am I Blue?: Coming Out from the Silence, 1994 (editor)

teacher helped to support him in his seminary studies. After her two children were born, she turned her attention to raising them. When her children were old enough to go to school, she and her husband agreed that she would spend five years trying to establish herself as a writer. If she failed, she would return to the classroom. Her first book, *Shelter from the Wind*, was published three years later, in 1976.

On My Honor, her sixth novel, won Bauer praise and attention. Based upon an actual event, the novel deals with one boy's guilt at having caused the accidental death of a friend. Joel, not knowing that his friend Tony is a poor swimmer, dares him to swim in a swiftly-moving river. Tony is pulled under the water and swept away. Joel, exhausted by his attempts to

Pacifism

Pacifism is the belief that differences should be negotiated through diplomacy and arbitration rather than through violence or war. A pacifist would not take up arms against another country, even if the security of his or her own country was threatened. In countries with required military service, pacifists might be given the opportunity to do alternative service such as delivering meals to the elderly or working in nursing homes. A person who refuses to serve in the military is called a concientious objector because his or her conscience will not allow the use of weapons for moral or religious reasons.

Homosexuality

Homosexuality is a term that defines people who are sexually attracted to members of the same sex. Heterosexuality is a term that defines people who are sexually attracted to members of the opposite sex. These words were first used by a Viennese writer and journalist, Karoly Maria Kertbeny, in 1869. The terms have continued to be used since that time. Today, gradual steps are being taken in many societies to offer homosexual men and women the same civil rights that heterosexuals enjoy. The six-colored Rainbow Flag, designed in 1978, is a symbol of gay and lesbian community pride.

rescue Tony, returns home, but does not tell anyone what has happened, as if pretending Tony is not dead will somehow return him to life. The novel received a **Newbery Honor Book** citation in 1987.

Marion Dane Bauer's work deals with actions, their consequences, and the difficulties people face when trying to live with integrity and compassion, both for themselves and others. In addition to her own writing she was the editor of *Am I Blue?: Coming Out from the Silence*, a collection of stories by different authors on gay and lesbian themes. That book helped bring the concerns of youths dealing with **homosexuality** to a wider audience.

– Angela M. Salas

.102

.57

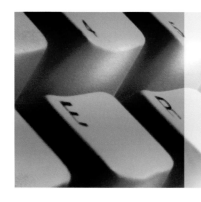

Nina Bawden

Born: January 19, 1925; London, England

www.ninabawden.net

Nina Bawden has long been a prolific writer of children's and adult novels. Her young adult novels deal with such issues as young people finding identity in dysfunctional or reconstituted families, transpositions to unfamiliar cultures, and intergenerational relationships. Although Bawden is a realistic writer, she is fascinated by the extraordinary in characters, cultures, and events. She keeps within traditional mystery plot frameworks, yet manages to find new twists.

Bawden was born in London, where her high-school education was interrupted by World War II, when her school was **evacuated** to South **Wales**. Her teenage experiences of the very alien life of Welsh mining villagers, and later, of the remote Shropshire countryside, provided her with plot material that she would later use in her books. After the war, she entered Somerville College at Oxford. After graduating she married H. W. Bawden, with whom she had two sons. The couple divorced, and she later married Austen Kark of the **British Broadcasting Corporation**, with whom she had a daughter. Her first adult novel was published in 1953. In addition to her many novels, she has also written *In My Own Times: Almost an Autobiography* in 1994.

Bawden's first young adult fiction book, *The House of Secrets*, introduces her recurring character types and plot elements: children displaced from a happy life in one culture (Africa in this book), to an unhappy and constricting situation in another. The novel was influenced greatly by Frances Burnett's

p.59

p.18

p.6

The Secret Garden (1911). The displacement is similarly resolved by finding another child even more unhappy, whom the children are able to help. *The Witch's Daughter* established Bawden as a gifted children's author. The members of an English family vacationing on a remote Scottish island befriend Perdita, an orphaned and reclusive girl who is believed to have second sight. In fact it is the blind English girl who saves them by being able to "see" in the dark. Together they reveal two criminals and their hidden loot. Perdita is integrated back into society as a "normal" child.

To many readers, *Carrie's War* is Bawden's best young adult fiction. In this novel, Carrie revisits the site of her wartime evacuation, a Welsh mining village. Happy and unhappy memories are revived as the narrative shifts back to her adolescent perceptions. A final visit to the burnt-out site of her happier memories absolves her from the guilt she long felt. She believed she had set off a curse in her anger at being caught up in the Welsh family's

Wartime Evacuation

During World War II, many families who lived in London and key port cities sent their children to live in more rural places or towns that were not heavily involved in to the war effort. Children lived with relatives, host families, or in group homes. During the Battle of Britain, in which German enemy aircraft made merciless attacks on English cities such as London and Coventry, some 1,000 civilians were killed in the bombings. The evacuated children were kept safe by moving them away from the cities.

Magistrate

A magistrate is a person appointed to act as a judge in a local British court. There are no formal requirements to be a magistrate. This is a part-time appointment. The magistrate's functions include listening to cases against adults and children which may result in a fine, public service, or probation. A magistrate also serves on committees and settles family problems.

feud, but in fact the outcome is resolved quite differently from what she imagined. Another book based on Bawden's wartime evacuation experiences is *Keeping Henry*, a delightful story of a red squirrel that is kept as a pet. The squirrel symbolizes the entrapment and freedom of various human characters in the story.

Bawden's other novels include stories dealing with adoptive or stepparents and half-brothers and sisters, such as *The Robbers*, *The Finding*, and *The Outside Child*. Stories dealing with grandparents and grandchildren include *The Real Plato Jones*, *Granny the Pag*, and *Off the Road*. Bawden has explored bolder themes concerning abused and terrorized children that draw on her experiences as a **magistrate**. These books include *Squib*, *Kept in the Dark*, and *Humbug*.

p.60

Nina Bawden's novels have received a number of citations. *Carrie's War* won the **Phoenix Award** p.147 of the Children's Literature Association in 1993. It was also the subject of a British Broadcasting Corporation television presentation, as was *The Witch's Daughter*. *Kept in the Dark* received a **Parents' Choice Award** in 1983, as did *The Finding* in 1985, p.153 while *The Peppermint Pig* was the **Guardian Award** winner for 1976.

– David Barratt

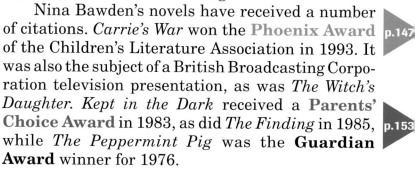

Patricia Beatty

Born: August 26, 1922; Portland, Oregon
Died: July 9, 1991; Riverside, California

Patricia Beatty loved history and strove to share her fascination with the past with her adolescent readers. A prolific author, she published fifty books under her own name and ten more with her first husband, John Beatty. While some of her collaborations with her husband were set in England, her own books reveal her preference for American history and her deep feelings for California, where she spent most of her life.

Good historical fiction demands careful research. Beatty was a librarian for many years and searched for details that would interest her readers and put life into her young male and female characters. Her writing notes outlined her research and distinguished between events in her stories that really happened and those that she created.

Many of Beatty's books are set during the 1860's. In *Wait for Me, Watch for Me, Eula Bee*, two children are captured by Comanche and Kiowa warriors and taken to their village. The older boy escapes, but the young girl remains and eventually becomes attached to her adopted Native American parent. As an adopted daughter of the Quileute people in western Washington, Beatty drew upon her first-hand knowledge of Native American culture.

The American Civil War is the backdrop for many of Beatty's novels, both directly and indirectly. In *Charley Skedaddle*, Charley Quinn is a tough gang member in New York City who joins the Union Army to avenge his brother's death at the hands of the Confederates. The reality of war terrifies him,

p.35

p.117

TITLES

Wait for Me, Watch for Me, Eula Bee, 1978

Eight Mules from Monterey, 1982

Turn Homeward, Hannalee, 1984

Charley Skedaddle, 1987

Be Ever Hopeful, Hannalee, 1988

Jayhawker, 1991

Who Comes with Cannons?, 1992

however, and he becomes "Charley Skedaddle" when he deserts into the Blue Ridge Mountains, where he faces a different set of challenges. This book won the Scott O'Dell Award for Historical Fiction. *Turn Homeward, Hannalee*, and its sequel, *Be Ever Hopeful, Hannalee*, trace the adventures of a young mill worker who is sent from her home in Georgia to work in Northern mills near the end of the Civil War. In *Jayhawker*, Lije Tulley spies on Confederates in Missouri and Kansas and carries on his father's abolitionist efforts. *Who Comes with Cannons*—which was published after Beatty died—is about a Quaker girl whose family helps slaves escape via the Underground Railroad.

p.63
p.51
p.749
p.255

The setting for *Eight Mules from Monterey* is twentieth century Northern California. During the summer of 1916, thirteen-year old Fayette Ashmore travels with her widowed mother and her brother into the mountains south of Monterey to set up library outposts. Accompanied by a mule-driver called Possum, the family deals with a number of interesting situations. Selected as a National Council for the Social Studies **Notable Children's Trade Book in the Field of Social Studies** (1983), this book combines Beatty's two loves—reading and history.

p.650

John and Patricia Beatty Award

The John and Patricia Beatty Award was first given in 1989 to the author of a young adult novel that promotes an awareness of California and its people. It is announced each year during National Library Week, and the prize of $500 and an engraved plaque is given to the winning author during the California Library Association convention in November. Patricia Beatty first funded the award in memory of her husband, who taught at the University of California at Riverside prior to his death in 1975. Patricia Beatty hoped the award would encourage authors to write high quality books and increase knowledge about California's past and future.

Shenandoah National Park

The Blue Ridge Mountains in the Southern Appalachian Mountains of Virginia were the site of a number of Civil War manuveurs by General Thomas J. "Stonewall" Jackson and his troops that benefited the Confederates. In 1935 the area was designated as Shenandoah National Park. The construction of Skyline Drive gave the public a road to travel through the park and the opportunity to view the beautiful mountain landscape or camp and picnic along the highway. The highway and its buildings, built during the Great Depression, are now listed on the National Register of Historic Places.

p.62

Patricia Beatty won many awards for her own novels, but in 1988 she created an award of her own: the **John and Patricia Beatty Award**. This honor is given each year by the California Library Association to a book that best promotes awareness of California and its people. Beatty's extensive body of work remains as an exciting way for adolescents to experience moments in America's past.

– Kay Moore

James Berry

Born: 1925; Fair Prospect, Jamaica

www.mystworld.com/youngwriter/authors/
jamesberry.html

Born in Jamaica, **James Berry** was one of six children who lived quite happily on a poor subsistence farm beside the sea. At an early age he was intrigued with learning about history and about what directed the course of human events. As a young man, he spent four years working in the United States during World War II. Disillusioned by how black people were treated in America, he returned to Jamaica after the war. In 1948 Berry emigrated to England, where he eventually gained recognition as a poet and short story writer whose mission was to use his Jamaican memories to record the stories of his people. Although he is best known for his poetry and short stories, his only novel was well received. p.65

Berry's first book for young readers, *A Thief in the Village and Other Stories*, was not published until almost forty years after he settled in England, where he worked as a telegrapher for many years. When his job was eliminated by automation, Berry retired with a pension that made it possible for him to become a full-time writer. Jamaica was one of the last bastions of the British Empire and, as such, was largely ignored in literature until Berry focused attention upon it. His books use the English language with remarkable accuracy and sensitivity, capturing well the cadences of **West Indian** folk tales, as in *Anancy, Spiderman*, whose main character is a **trickster**, a crafty character legendary in West Indian folklore. p.671

p.414

Berry's widely read novel *Ajeemah and His Son*

is set in Africa in 1807, when Ajeemah and his son, Atu, travel from their home to deliver a dowry of two gold pieces to Sisi, the woman Atu plans to marry. Along the way, both father and son are captured by slave traders who hustle them onto a ship bound for Jamaica and sell them into slavery. Although the two are purchased by plantation owners whose properties are near each other, neither ever sees the other again. Both Ajeemah and Atu struggle to maintain their dignity in the face of devastating circumstances. Ajeemah finally lets go of his African roots and remarries. Ultimately, he gains his freedom when all the slaves in the British Empire are freed in 1834. However, emancipation comes too late for Atu, who has grown so bitter that he commits suicide.

Jamaica

Jamaica, about the size of the state of Connecticut, is the third largest island in the Caribbean Sea. Its capital, Kingston, is the largest English-speaking city south of Miami, Florida. Its varied and painful history was particularly marked by British colonization during the 17th century and the importation of African slaves to work the profitable sugar plantations. Slavery was abolished in 1834. Jamaica gained independence in 1962 and remains a member of the Commonwealth. Jamaica is now one of the world's largest suppliers of bauxite, or aluminum ore. In addition to the mining of bauxite, its largest industry is tourism. Among Jamaica's internationally known resort areas are Montego Bay and Ocho Rios. The population of Jamaica is more than 2.5 million people, of whom 91% are black.

In eighty-three tightly packed pages, James Berry relates this complex story in vivid detail, his prose brimming with the emotion that the situation naturally evokes. Berry stumbled upon the idea for this novel by recalling that in his childhood, he and his six siblings had played on the ruins of a sugar mill on a former slave plantation. The details of slavery in the West Indies had not previously been dealt with in literature. In 1993, this novel earned Berry both the **Coretta Scott King Award** and the **Boston Globe-Horn Book Award**.

 p.66

p.747

– R. Baird Shuman

Coretta Scott King Award

Established in 1967, the Coretta Scott King Award is given each year to one author and one illustrator of African descent whose books help readers understand and appreciate the "American Dream." It honors the life and work of Dr. Martin Luther King, Jr., and the continuing peace efforts of his widow. Winners receive a framed citation, a cash prize, and an encyclopedia set. The award is presented by the Coretta Scott King Task Force of the American Library Association's Ethnic Multicultural Information Exchange Round Table.

Francesca Lia Block

Born: December 3, 1962; Hollywood, California

www.francescaliablock.com

Francesca Lia Block has won critical acclaim for her books depicting the youth subculture. Her novels have aroused criticism because of their treatment of controversial topics such as, sex, homosexuality and drug use among teenagers. However, her real message is the power of love, the triumphant force that connects us all together and elevates us above our circumstances. Her style fascinates readers as well, offering a dazzling blend of folklore and magic and super-hip characters. Her own magical sensibility attracts a cult-like following among young readers and adults alike.

Block was born and raised in Los Angeles, California. Her father was a painter and teacher and her mother a poet. As a child, Block was an avid reader and wrote stories and poems. While a student at North Hollywood High School, she enjoyed cruising around nearby Hollywood with friends, exploring its punk culture. She continued her formal education at the University of California at Berkeley and began writing fiction. Returning to Los Angeles, she wrote book-review essays and taught writing workshops.

Many of Block's fictional characters are eccentric misfits who experience abandonment, disloyalty, and abuse but eventually find the strength to survive through love and creative expression.

p.68

TITLES

Weetzie Bat, 1989

Witch Baby, 1991

Cherokee Bat and the Goat Guys, 1992

Missing Angel Juan, 1993

The Hanged Man, 1994

Baby Be-Bop, 1995

Girl Goddess #9: Nine Stories, 1996

Dangerous Angels: The Weetzie Bat Books, 1998

I Was a Teenage Fairy, 1998

Violet and Claire, 1999

The Rose and the Beast, 2000

Echo, 2001

Wasteland, 2003

Primavera, 2004

FRANCESCA LIA BLOCK

67

Punk Music

Punk music was born of the no-frills garage bands of the 1960's. They played simple three-chord rock and roll with buzz-saw guitars, pounding drums, and often angry lyrics. New York City was the center of the punk movement in the early 1970's. A club in the Bowery called CBGB presented such bands as Television, the Talking Heads, soloist Patti Smith, and the Ramones for their first public performances. The Ramones appearance in London in 1976 gave the English punk scene a boost. Malcolm McLaren had formed the English group the Sex Pistols in 1975, and they were to give the movement its characteristics: spiked hair, black leather clothing, and rude behavior.

In *Weetzie Bat*, Block's first novel, Weetzie lives in Los Angeles with a gay friend, Dirk. She meets My Secret Lover Man, who brings with him Witch Baby from a former relationship, and they have a child named Cherokee together. Their fairy-tale life is filled with love and magic, including a genie.

In Block's next novel, *Witch Baby*, the title character searches for understanding and acceptance, which come to her when she finds her real mother. In *Cherokee Bat and the Goat Guys*, Cherokee and Witch Baby form a band with two friends. The band's success depends on magical gifts from Coyote, a Native American. *Missing Angel Juan* shifts the action to New York City, where Witch Baby searches for Angel Juan with the help of her grandfather's ghost. In *The Hanged Man*, a young woman struggles with her emotions after the death of her father, with whom she has had an incestuous relationship. *Baby Be-Bop* focuses on Dirk's life before he meets Weetzie and while he is still dealing with the realization that he is gay. In *I Was a Teenage Fairy*, eleven-year-old Barbie is pushed into modeling by her mother and is molested by a photographer. *Violet and Claire* explores the relationship of an ambitious seventeen-year-old screenwriter and her friend, a passive young woman who is a poet. In *Echo*, the title character is ignored by her parents and ultimately realizes that she must look inside herself for the power to survive. *Wasteland* tells the story of a loving but inappropriate relationship between brother Lex and his sister, Marina; and in *Primavera*, the title character goes in search of the magical city of Elysia by motorcycle.

Francesca Block has also written two volumes of poetry, a collection of short stories (*Girl Goddess #9*), screenplays, and novels for adults. *Necklace of Kisses*, to be published in Fall 2005, features Weetzie at age forty. In 1986 Block received the **Shrout Short Story Prize** for her short fiction. The American Library Association awarded her **Best Book for Young Adults** for the years 1989 and 1990 and each year from 1992 to 1996. **Best Books of the Year** citations also came from *School Library Journal* in 1991 and from the *New York Times* and *Publisher's Weekly* in 1992. In 1995 the **American Library Association** also awarded Block the **Lesbian and Bisexual Book Award**.

p.69
p.480
p.195
p.144
p.45

– Bernard E. Morris

Shrout Short Story Prize

The Shrout Short Story Prize is given each year for the best short story written by a student at the University of California at Berkeley. It was established in 1943, when the university sold two lots that were left in the will of Julia Keith Shrout for the purpose of establishing a memorial fund. Shrout stipulated that the university should wait until the lots were worth $2,500, but the court indicated that the university could either keep the lots or sell them for fair market value. The lots were sold for $200. The university adds to the memorial fund in order to award the $400 prize.

Edward Bloor

Born: October 12, 1950; Trenton, New Jersey

www.readin.org/authors/author_pages/bloor/
bloor.htm

Using bold strokes, **Edward Bloor** portrays courageous teens enmeshed in confusing and dangerous situations that require inventive action to ensure survival. Through a series of complicated events, the stories reveal the unexpected strengths of their misfit protagonists. Bloor's young characters battle to overcome dysfunctional families, lack of acceptance by their peers, and self-doubt. Additional social and environmental issues threaten their safety and happiness.

p.233

Growing up in New Jersey, Bloor became an avid reader at an early age and soon realized that he could also write stories to entertain his family and peers. He enjoyed reading sports novels and playing basketball, soccer, baseball, and football. When he was in the seventh grade, he wrote comedy skits that he and his friends performed. Later his writing career received a brief setback when he paid an editing house to publish his first novel. The disreputable firm kept his money but did not publish the book.

During the 1980's Bloor became a teacher and then an editor. Reading young adult novels on the job encouraged him to try writing similar books of his own. He began the process by observing his surroundings in a citrus-growing region of Florida.

p.2(

Bloor's first book, *Tangerine*, features a disabled soccer-playing protagonist caught up in a mystery. Seventh-grader Paul Fisher wears big glasses and is nearly blind, a result of eye damage caused under mysterious circumstances when he was a young child. He has been told that he was nearly

Solar Eclipse

A solar eclipse occurs when the moon passes between the Sun and the earth and the moon's shadow falls on the earth. The Sun appears to go dark for a few minutes, with a halo of light shining from the edge of the black disc. The Sun can only be safely viewed with the naked eye during the brief seconds of a total solar eclipse. It is never safe to watch a partial eclipse without taking special care. An eclipse can be viewed by projection. A pinhole or small opening is used to cast the image of the Sun on a screen placed a few feet away. You also can purchase filters designed for this purpose. Attempting to watch the partial eclipse with the naked eye can cause permanent eye damage or blindness.

blinded from staring too long at an **eclipse**, but he suspects that there is something about his accident that his parents are not telling him, and that they may be covering up for something his cruel older brother, Erik did. Erik is a high-school football hero and the pride and joy of the family Meanwhile, Paul can play soccer when he wears special goggles.

The Fisher family has recently moved to Florida. They soon discover that their new neighborhood is plagued by smoke clouds from muck fires in a nearby swamp and by daily lightning storms. Paul struggles not only to avoid Erik but also to win a place on the soccer team and to fit in at his new school, but strange and life-threatening events intervene.

In Bloor's next novel, *Crusader*, Roberta Ritter is impressed with a new virtual reality war game, although she has no plans to play the game itself. She works at the Arcane, their family-owned and nearly bankrupt arcade at a crummy mall. Roberta wants

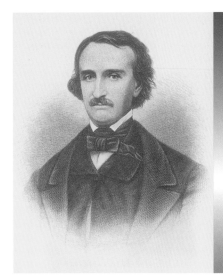

Edgar Allan Poe Award for Best Young Adult Novel

The Mystery Writers of America was founded in 1945 by a group of writers to help promote mystery writing. The group gives a number of Edgar Awards each year, named for the "Father of the Detective Story," the 19th century writer Edgar Allan Poe. The category of Young Adult was added in 1989. The winner receives a small bust of Poe.

to know why her mother was murdered in the arcade seven years earlier. She is resolved to solve this mystery, and her father's romance with the mall manager simply adds to Roberta's resolve. Hate-crime allegations, a suicide, and corrupt local politicians add complexity to the story. Only one friend truly believes in Roberta's capabilities to uncover the truth. Few imagine that the immature-looking fifteen-year-old is ingenious enough to unravel the web of trouble she faces. *Crusader* rings true to life in a world where winning or losing involves more hurt and happiness than can be derived from the killing of computer-generated enemies.

Bloor's third novel, *Story Time*, pits two clever characters, eighth-grader Katie and sixth-grader George, against their highly "controlled" and standardized-test-driven Whittaker Magnet School. It blends humor and fantasy with a satire of modern U.S. education.

Bloor's first novel *Tangerine* was listed in the American Library Association's **Top Ten Young Adult Book** list and was nominated for the **Edgar Allan Poe Award for Best Young Adult Novel** the same year.

p.72
p.45

– Margaret A. Dodson

Judy Blume

Born: February 12, 1938; Elizabeth, New Jersey
www.judyblume.com

Popular yet controversial, the works of **Judy Blume** span several decades, but their timeless appeal rests in Blume's ability to portray accurately the emotional lives of her young characters. Her novels explore social and ethical problems that sometimes cause discomfort among parents and teachers of her readers. Some of her books have been **banned** from libraries and schools due to their frank treatment of death, spirituality, divorce, and emerging sexuality. At the same time, however, her books are light-hearted and full of positive examples and humorous adventures.

p.10
p.74

Judy (Sussman) Kitchens Blume was born in New Jersey, the daughter of a dentist father and an attorney mother. Many of her books, some of which are semi-autobiographical, are set in New Jersey as a result of her early experiences there. She graduated from New York University, where she took her first writing class and her teacher encouraged her to continue writing realistic stories. Blume has said she has always loved books, and that writing about young people comes naturally to her because she has almost total recall of everything that happened to her since third grade. She is the mother of two children, and her own divorce became the inspiration for her writing as well.

Blume's characters often confront fearful situations, such as divorce and death, and grow as a result. In *Otherwise Known as Sheila the Great*, Sheila is afraid of everything: attics, thunderstorms, even a stained-glass window in a church near her home.

TITLES

Are You There God? It's Me, Margaret, 1970

Freckle Juice, 1971

Then Again, Maybe I Won't, 1971

It's Not the End of the World, 1972

Otherwise Known as Sheila the Great, 1972

Tales of a Fourth Grade Nothing, 1972

Blubber, 1974

Starring Sally J. Freedman as Herself, 1977

Superfudge, 1980

Tiger Eyes, 1981

Characters in Blume's other books face more serious fears. In *Starring Sally J. Freedman as Herself*, a work Blume considers to be her most autobiographical, Sally worries that her forty-two-year-old father will die because two of her uncles died when they were his age. She establishes an elaborate prayer ritual, asking God to allow her father to live. When Sally finally talks to her father about her fears, she finds that he shares her worries. In *Tiger Eyes*, the main character, Davey Wexler, is also haunted by

Banned Books Week

Held every September since 1981, Banned Books Week is sponsored by the American Library Association, American Booksellers Association, American Society of Journalists and Authors, Association of American Publishers, National Association of College Stores, and the American Association of University Presses to celebrate the freedom to read and call public attention to censorship. Books that have been censored throughout history include *The Bible*, Brothers Grimm fairy tales, *The American Heritage Dictionary*, *The Wizard of Oz*, *The Adventures of Huckleberry Finn*, *Catch 22*, and *The Grapes of Wrath*.

KIDS Fund

In 1981, Judy Blume started KIDS Fund as a way to encourage better communication between parents and their children. She gave the royalties from sales of *The Judy Blume Diary* (1981), a book with quotes from Blume's works, photographs, and blank pages for fans to create their own twelve month diaries, to the KIDS Fund and has donated some $40,000 a year to a variety of non-profit organizations.

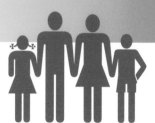

fear. Davey's father dies after being shot in a robbery, and fifteen-year-old Davey is overcome by grief and fear. No one understands her feelings, and she sleeps with a bread knife under her pillow. She struggles to break free of the paralysis of fear and eventually determines to live without fear.

Since divorce, too, causes grief, fear, and a sense of tragic loss among the children whom it affects, Blume wrote *It's Not the End of the World* as she was recovering from her own divorce. The reactions of her central character, Karen, reveal the difficulty of explaining to a child the complex issues that are involved in divorce.

Although almost all of Judy Blume's books have been censored at one time or another over the years, her works have received numerous awards. In 2004, four of her most popular books—*Are You There God? It's Me, Margaret*; *Tales of a Fourth Grade Nothing*; *Otherwise Known as Sheila the Great*; and *Blubber*—were acknowledged for selling more than 20 million copies combined. Blume was given the National Book Foundation Medal for Distinguished Contribution to American Letters.

– Kathleen M. Bartlett

Cecil Bodker

Born: March 27, 1927; Fredericia, Denmark

Characters in **Cecil Bodker**'s books for young readers are either black or white, wholly evil or remarkably good. However, most fall into the latter category, which is what gives her stories their dramatic tension. In most of Bodker's stories, adults are the enemy. This characterization endears this author to troubled youths who are in one way or another coping with the kinds of problems about which she writes. All of Bodker's writing is characterized by the speed with which her narration moves. This quality has enticed many reluctant readers to become devotees of Bodker's young adult novels.

Born in Denmark, Bodker is the daughter of author and artist H. P. Jacobsen and his wife, Gertrude. She became a silversmith in her early twenties and worked in that capacity until 1952. She was raised with four brothers and for a time was the only woman in a silversmith **apprenticeship** with some fifty men. It is, therefore, not surprising that the **protagonists** in her stories are exclusively male.

p.233
p.246

In 1969 Bodker accepted an invitation from the **Ethiopian** government to live in that country and to write something about life in Ethiopia specifically for Ethiopian children. The result was her young adult novel *The Leopard*, which received an award from the **American Library Association** in 1977. This fast-paced book places its protagonist, Tibesco, in a variety of rapidly changing scenes and circumstances that engage young readers. Tibesco is not particularly courageous but prevails because he is resolute as he faces his problems. The story moves

p.77
p.45

quickly from mountain village to bustling town to the lively river bank, an Ethiopian gathering place. Bodker employs the local dialect to reflect Tibesco's psychological reactions to the many situations and places that affect his life. Bodker's use of the local language captures the dynamics of life in remote Ethiopian towns.

Bodker is best known to English-speaking readers for her Silas trilogy, which is made up of *Silas and the Black Mare*, *Silas and Ben-Godik*, and *Silas and the Runaway Coach*. Silas is a prototype of the **picaresque** protagonist. Always male, picaresque heroes get themselves into menacing situations but escape by facing their dangers and using their wits. Bodker's Silas stands in sharp contrast to Tibesco, who is basically cowardly but who prevails through sheer persistence.

Bodker's writing has often been compared to that of Franz Kafka and Jerzy Kosinski. This comparison is especially true of the Silas stories in which young Silas runs away from his family of

Ethiopia

Ethiopia is a landlocked African country that is among the poorest in the world. The majority of the population grows crops. However, the expanding Sahara Desert and the frequent drought conditions make farming difficult. Since the time that Bodker lived in Ethiopia, the country has been hard hit with political turmoil, and Ethiopia has become locked in a battle with neighboring country Eritrea, which was separated from Ethiopia by Italian occupiers in the late 1930's. This has forced the movement of people from one territory to another and created further chaos and famine.

traveling circus performers and encounters an incredible combination of cruel and deceitful people who are out cheat him, beat him, or worse.

In 1967 the **Danish Academy** bestowed upon Cecil Bodker the only prize it ever awarded for a work of young adult literature, *Silas and the Black Mare*, published in English translation eleven years later. Bodker received the **Brachmann Prize** for her writing in 1973, the **Hans Christian Andersen Medal** in 1976, and the **Mildred Batchelder Award** in 1977.

 p.120

p.468

– R. Baird Shuman

Picaro

A *picaro* is the main character in a *picaresque*, a type of story that emerged in sixteenth century Spain, the best example being *Lazarillo de Tormes*. He is always a low-life character who travels from master to master in search of financial stability. While he learns to survive, he does not change. Pressured by circumstances to chose between integrity and survival, the *picaro* makes the practical choice and learns to adjust to the corrupt values of his environment.

PENGUIN CLASSICS

Lazarillo de Tormes and *The Swindler:*
Two Spanish Picaresque Novels

Nancy Bond

Born: January 8, 1945; Bethesda, Maryland

www.concordnet.org/library/scollect/Fin_Aids/Bond.html

Nancy Bond writes about relationships, the difficulties of friendship, and the importance of family. Her novels explore the varying ways in which individuals see and solve problems. Her themes are not new, she says, but the way she approaches them is her own.

Born in Maryland, Bond grew up during the 1950's in a secure family. She had few playmates, so she read a great deal. She found friends in books and invented stories of her own. As a child, she was never eager for change but came to realize that change is unavoidable. She would later make it a central theme in her books.

A lifelong lover of England and its people, Bond moved to London, England, at the age of eight when her father was studying on a **Fulbright Scholarship**. She returned to the British Isles many times after that and has used British characters and settings in several of her novels. Her first book, *A String in the Harp*, is set in **Wales**. She wrote it after **studying librarianship** in Aberystwyth, Wales, during the early 1970's. The book is the story of young Peter Morgan and his two sisters. They move to Wales, where their father has accepted a new job. While grieving the loss of his mother, Peter finds a harp key that belonged to the sixth century Welsh bard Taliesin; afterward, he begins to experience important events in Taliesin's life. Slipping deeper into his fantasy—or perhaps an alternate reality—Peter withdraws from his family. Only the key can reunite them.

p.80

p.18

134

TITLES

A String in the Harp, 1976

The Best of Enemies, 1978

Country of Broken Stone, 1980

The Voyage Begun, 1981

A Place to Come Back To, 1984

Another Shore, 1988

Truth to Tell, 1994

The Love of Friends, 1997

The theme of families in crisis recurs in several other works. In *Truth to Tell*, fourteen-year-old Alice reluctantly moves to **New Zealand** with her mother. There she confronts the mystery of her father's alleged death. In *Country of Broken Stone*, a divorced mother and a widowed father marry and move to England's Northumbria region. Their children must cope with the harsh weather and stark countryside of their new home, while overcoming the problems inherent in forging one family from two.

p.456

The potentials and perils of teenage friendship are probed in several of Bond's books. A trilogy explores the relationship of Charlotte Paige and Oliver Shattuck. In *The Best of Enemies*, twelve-year-old Charlotte looks forward to Patriots' Day celebration in Concord, only to see it spoiled by a conflict with modern-day Loyalists, including Oliver. In the second novel, *A Place to Come Back To*, the death of his great-uncle throws Oliver into despondency, placing emotional demands on Charlotte that she has trouble meeting. In the third book, *The Love of Friends*, Oliver persuades Charlotte to accompany him to Scotland. The journey leads them to learn about making decisions and taking responsibility.

Some of Bond's novels employ fantasy and science-fiction elements. In *Another Shore*, seventeen-year-old Lyn Paget works as a costumed guide

p.87

Fulbright Scholarship

The Fulbright Program was introduced in 1946 by Senator J. William Fulbright. Since that time, more than 255,000 U.S. and foreign students have participated, with U.S. students studying at universities in participating countries and foreign students studying at universities in the U.S.A. The scholarships are funded by Congress to the Department of State. Participating governments and universities also share in the costs. The purpose of the program is to create better understanding and cooperation by exposing individuals to other cultures and peoples.

Fossil Fuels

Fossil fuels such as coal, oil, and natural gas are the primary fuel sources for the industrial nations of the world. Developing nations that are trying to raise their standard of living by becoming more industrialized are also using more fossil fuels. As this use has increased, so has the awareness that fossil fuels will eventually be depleted and that they produce pollution in the atmosphere when they are burned.

in the historical reproduction of a Nova Scotia port city. After suddenly finding herself in the year 1744, she must avoid the hazards of eighteenth century life while searching for a way to return to her own time. *The Voyage Begun* is set in the near future when fossil fuels are depleted. Climate change and environmental pollution have turned the once-thriving communities around Cape Cod into ghost towns.

Nancy Bond has won many awards for her books. *A String in the Harp* was a 1977 Newbery Honor Book. It also won the International Reading Association's Children's Book Award that same year and the Welsh Arts Council's Tir na Og Award. *Country of the Broken Stone* was a 1980 *Booklist* Reviewers' Choice book. *The Voyage Begun* was a 1982 Boston Globe-Horn Book Honor Book.

– Faith Hickman Brynie

.81

102

143

p.621

p.747

Malcolm Bosse, Jr.

Born: May 6, 1933; Detroit, Michigan
Died: May 3, 2002; New York, New York

Malcolm Bosse is generally praised for the vividness of his writing. He views any reader over twelve as an adult. His books, therefore, do not condescend in any way to his juvenile audience.

Born in Michigan, Bosse earned a bachelor of arts degree at Yale University in 1950, a master's degree from the University of Michigan in 1956, and a doctorate in English from New York University in 1969. That year he began his tenure as a professor of English at the City University of New York.

Bosse's first work of young adult fiction, written after he had established himself as a novelist, was *The Seventy-nine Squares*, a novel about how fourteen-year-old Eric Fisher, on probation for minor misdeeds, is redeemed through befriending Mr. Beck, an eighty-two-year old man who has just been released after forty years in prison for killing his wife and who is dying of cancer. Beck has returned to his cherished garden, which he now has Eric divide into seventy-nine squares. Eric is to spend time studying the life of each square. Through this process, Eric comes to appreciate existence as he had never appreciated it before.

Bosse's next young adult novel, *Cave Beyond Time*, recounts how a disenchanted fifteen-year-old boy named Ben is bitten by a rattlesnake while on an **archaeological dig** in Arizona. The story recounts his delirium, during which he imagines himself to be a nomad and a prehistoric hunter. This novel re-

 p.83

ceived an award from the **National Council for the Social Studies** in 1981.

During two years spent as a lecturer in India, Bosse garnered the material for *Ganesh*, the name of the elephant-headed Hindu god of strength and wisdom, and also the nickname of the book's main character Jeffrey Moore, born in the United States but raised in India. When both of Jeffrey's parents die during his fifteenth year, he is sent to live with his Aunt Betty in the American Midwest, where he is shunned because of his foreign mannerisms. In the end, however, he thwarts a government attempt to run a road through his aunt's home, using principles of **passive resistance** he learned in India. He thereby wins the respect of his peers. This novel was named the most notable juvenile trade book in social studies.

.84

p.327

In *Captives of Time*, Bosse writes about Anne and Niklas Valens, children who are forced to travel across plague-ridden medieval Europe to find their uncle af-

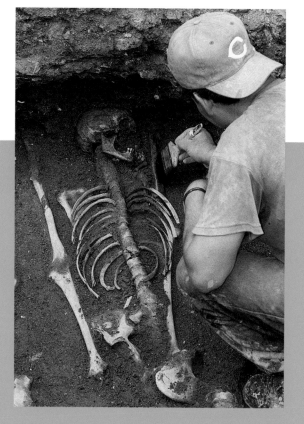

Archaeological Dig

Archaeology is the scientific study of the material remains, such as fossils, tools, religious items, and structures, of past human life and activities. In order to uncover the remains of earlier cultures, it is often necessary to dig. A site that is being uncovered is called an archaeological dig. Trained archaeologists work at sites all around the world and even under the sea. The items they discover tell archaeologists much about how early peoples lived, what foods they ate, how they obtained their food, how they died, and so on. An archaeological dig must be planned and executed very carefully to avoid destroying any scientific evidence.

MALCOLM BOSSE, JR.

Nonviolent Resistance

India's Mohandas Gandhi was known for his policy of nonviolent resistance. This Indian leader led several national protests against the British colonial rulers. One of the most famous was his protest against the Salt Laws, which banned the sale and manufacture of

salt in India. When his letters to the British Viceroy went unanswered, he led seventy-eight of his followers on a march to the coast. After twenty-four days, Gandhi arrived at the coast and picked up a small handful of salt. All over India, people began making, buying, and selling salt. The British jailed more than sixty thousand people, including Gandhi. Even when the police were violent, the people resisted nonviolently. The final result was that Gandhi met with the British and the Salt Law was ended.

ter the murder of their parents. For his next two young adult novels, Bosse returned to Asia. Both *Deep Dream of the Rain Forest* and *The Examination* are about young men. The former novel recounts the story of a fifteen-year-old boy who becomes involved in following the quest of a tribesman from Borneo. In *The Examination*, brothers Hong and Chen, during the sixteenth century, journey across part of China to Beijing, where Chen must take a civil-service examination. Hong acts as his bodyguard on this trip that involves such hazards as a pirate attack and several clandestine missions.

– R. Baird Shuman

L. M. Boston

Born: December 10, 1892; Southport, Lancashire, England
Died: May 25, 1990; Hemingford Grey, Huntingdonshire, England
www.literatureforkids.com/kids/boston.html

Most of **L. M. Boston**'s young adult fiction is set around old English houses, especially the house of Green Knowe. Through the genre of time fantasy, Boston shows the living quality of the past in these houses, and the solidity of tradition in an alien and displaced world. Her beautiful descriptions of the English countryside lead to wider themes of the need for conservation and **preservation**.

Lucy Maria Boston was born into a strict religious family. After attending schools in England and Paris, France, she went on to Somerville College, Oxford, before becoming a nurse in World War I. In 1917 she married her cousin Harold, with whom she had one son, Peter, who was later to **illustrate** all but two of her children's books. The marriage was dissolved in 1935, after which Boston bought The Manor, a rambling old house dating back to the twelfth century, in the village of Hemingford Grey, Huntingdonshire, near Cambridge. From 1939 to 1945 she restored the house with help from her son. This house became "Green Knowe" in her fiction.

Boston did not start writing until she was nearly sixty years old, and was sixty-two when her first two novels were published; one was an adult novel, the other a young adult novel. Four further novels based on Green Knowe followed immediately; then six novellas, incorporating some of the same themes but in other settings; to be followed by her final children's fiction, a sixth book based on Green Knowe.

With one exception, the Green Knowe novels

.87
.86
p.38

TITLES

The Children of Green Knowe, 1954

Treasure of Green Knowe, 1958 (publ. in England as The Chimneys of Green Know)

The River at Green Knowe, 1959

A Stranger at Green Knowe, 1961

An Enemy at Green Knowe, 1964

The Castle of Yew, 1965

The Sea Egg, 1967

The House That Grew, 1969

Nothing Said, 1971

The Fossil Snake, 1973

The Guardians of the House, 1974

The Stones of Green Knowe, 1976

p.117

are historical fantasy. In *The Children of Green Knowe* a young boy nicknamed Tolly returns from Burma to his great-grandmother Oldknow's ancestral house. He connects with three children of a previous generation who died in the plague of 1665. He also connects with incidents in the eighteenth century when a curse was put on the family. Tolly helps break the curse at the same time as finding a true sense of belonging and family.

Tolly returns in *Treasure of Green Knowe*, this time reconnecting with the house's early nineteenth century inhabitants to find missing jewels that are worth enough to pay for much-needed repairs to the present structure. In *The River at Green Knowe*, other children become protagonists. However, p.233 they, like Tolly, are all displaced and need to find a sense of home. In the one nonfantasy title of the series, *A Stranger at Green Knowe*, Boston widens the theme of displacement to include a massive escaped gorilla who finally allows himself to be shot rather than return to captivity.

Boston's novellas are more subtly fantasy stories, continuing the setting of mysterious old houses and gardens, full of mythic presences, often with the idea of guardianship against the intruding forces of modernity. Interestingly, Boston's own favorite novella was *The Sea Egg*, the one story not about

National Trust for Historic Preservation

In the U.S., the National Trust for Historic Preservation leads the movement to save historic buildings and neigborhoods from being destroyed. Preserving these sites keeps history alive and allows us to remember and understand the past. The National Trust was founded in 1949 and took responsibility for its first site, Woodlawn Plantation in northern Virginia, in 1951. In addition to its role educating the public, the National Trust now manages a collection of 21 historic sites in the U.S.

Fantasy Literature

The fantastic in literature has been described by a famous literary critic, Tzvetan Todorov, as a genre that lies between the uncanny and the marvelous. While the marvelous presents an event that cannot be explained by the laws of the natural world and the uncanny presents an event that is the result of hallucination or illusion, the fantastic exists as long as the reader cannot decide which of these two applies.

houses but set in the magical Cornish coastline of southwest England.

Although L. M. Boston started writing late in her life, her achievements were recognized immediately. In 1955 *The Children of Green Knowe* was chosen as a **Distinguished Book** by the American Library Association, and in 1969 received the **Lewis Carroll Shelf Award**. *A Stranger at Green Knowe* won the **Carnegie Medal** in 1961 and was nominated a **Notable Book** by the American Library Association. p.45 p.42 p.45

– David Barratt

Candy Dawson Boyd

Born: August 8, 1946; Chicago, Illinois

p.233

p.401

p.89

Candy Dawson Boyd is best known for her portrayal of strong, three-dimensional African American **protagonists**. She derives much of her material from her own experiences growing up. The schools she attended as a child were **segregated**, but her family instilled in her an appreciation of their rich African American heritage. Impressed with how her ancestors had survived and prevailed in the face of adversity, she carried this message into her work as a field staff organizer with Martin Luther King, Jr.'s **Southern Christian Leadership Conference** in the 1960's.

After earning a college degree in education, Boyd worked as a classroom teacher in both Illinois and California, where she taught children from diverse ethnic backgrounds. She became dissatisfied with the children's books available for her students to read because few of them depicted nonwhite children in realistic situations. After spending two years reading numerous children's books, she decided to start writing the fiction she thought was missing. Her first published novel was *Circle of Gold*, the story of ten-year-old Mattie Benson who must cope with the death of her father and a faltering relationship with her mother. An argument with a classmate and a charge of theft hang over Mattie's head, but she is determined to earn enough money to buy her mother a valuable gift.

When Boyd became a college professor of education and a teacher trainer in reading and communications, she continued writing, using academic challenges and classroom situations as important plot elements in her books. For example, in *Breadsticks and Blessing Places*, twelve-year-old Toni Douglas struggles with sixth-grade math. When one of her

p.53

friends is killed by a **drunk driver**, Toni must overcome her grief and face a rigorous entrance exam for admission to a prep school. Boyd did extensive research on how children experience grief while writing this story.

In several of Boyd's books, a recurring theme is triumph in the face of obstacles, whether racial, interpersonal, or academic. Her strong characters are determined and resourceful. *Charlie Pippin* is the story of an eleven-year-old girl who gets in trouble at school. At home, she struggles to understand the despondency of her father, a disillusioned **Vietnam**

p.90

War veteran. Her efforts to complete a school project about the war despite her father's forced silence lead her to a broader understanding of both personal and societal conflicts.

Conflicts at school and at home figure into Boyd's other novels, such as *Chevrolet Saturdays*, in which fifth-grader Joey Davis finds himself at odds with a teacher, a classmate, and a new stepfather. The novel explores the challenges children face in forming new family relationships after divorce and remarriage. In *Fall Secrets*, Jessie, a sixth-grade

Southern Christian Leadership Conference

The Southern Christian Leadership Conference (SCLC) was formed in 1957 to help direct the growing movement among African Americans to gain equal civil rights. Martin Luther King, Jr., and more than sixty other ministers met in Atlanta, Georgia, to form the organization that would coordinate the movement. Its goal was to encourage nonviolent action to end segregation and discrimination in the South. From the beginning until King's assassination in 1968, the SCLC was one of the most effective organizations in the Civil Rights movement.

MARTIN LUTHER KING, JR.,
Founding President, SCLC

The Vietnam War

The U.S. was drawn into the politics of Vietnam in 1955, motivated by a desire to stop Communism from defeating democracy in South East Asia. North Vietnam, led by the popular Communist leader Ho Chi Minh, began armed attacks against U.S. soldiers and South Vietnamese troops as early as 1959, but it was not until the U.S. Congress passed the Gulf of Tonkin resolution in 1964 that then President Lyndon Johnson was given free hand to begin a build up of U.S. troops in Vietnam. By 1968 there were 550,000 U.S. troops in Vietnam. With the war going badly, President Richard Nixon introduced the strategy of Vietnamization in 1969, meaning getting the U.S. out of the country and turning the fighting over to the Vietnamese. In 1973, the final American forces withdrew from Vietnam. The U.S. had been unable to drive the Communists out of the South. The U.S. had the might but not the strategy to defeat the enemy. This war divided Americans and left many who fought in Vietnam feeling betrayed by their leaders and the American public.

girl, enters a middle school for the **performing arts**. p.242 Plagued with self-doubts about her skin color and appearance, she nevertheless comes to appreciate her personal worth and to take pride in her African American heritage. In the sequel, *A Different Beat*, Jessie faces a racially prejudiced teacher, but proves that she can succeed in her academic work and in her relationships with family and friends.

Candy Boyd has won numerous awards for her novels. *Circle of Gold* was honored by the **National Council for the Social Studies** and by the **Children's Book Council**. It was a **Coretta Scott King Award Honor Book** in 1985. *Charlie Pippin* p.66 was nominated for the **Mark Twain Award** and the **Dorothy Canfield Fisher Children's Book Award** in 1988.

– Faith Hickman Brynie

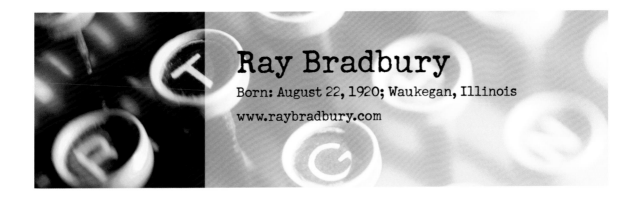

Ray Bradbury

Born: August 22, 1920; Waukegan, Illinois

www.raybradbury.com

p.87
p.92
p.233

Ray Bradbury has been one of the leading American writers of science fiction and fantasy for more than half a century, during which time he has helped revolutionize both of those genres. During the first half of the twentieth century, science-fiction and fantasy authors tended to rely heavily on the established stylistic conventions of popular, or **"pulp,"** **literature**, largely American Westerns and adventure stories. Bradbury introduced a new approach: storytelling that concentrated less on traditional hero-and-villain confrontations and more on the personal, internal struggles of his stories' **protagonists**. As a result, his short fiction has often been included in textbooks alongside authors of older "classics," such as Anton Chekhov and Nathaniel Hawthorne.

Bradbury grew up in a close extended family in a small Illinois town that he would call "Greentown," a place of refuge and belonging, in many of his novels and stories. In 1934 he moved with his family to Los Angeles, California, where he became fascinated by the world of film and theater. He joined his school drama club and dreamed of being an actor, until two influential English teachers helped redirect his focus to areas where they thought he had the greatest talent: writing fiction and poetry.

TITLES

The Martian Chronicles, 1950

The Illustrated Man, 1951

Fahrenheit 451, 1953

Dandelion Wine, 1957

Something Wicked This Way Comes, 1962

I Sing the Body Electric!, 1969

Pulp Literature

Pulp literature is the term applied to stories that, according to critics, have little literary value. They traditionally were science fiction, adventure, western, romance, hero, or war stories. The stories do not worry about character development or motivation. They are more concerned

with action. Many of these stories were first published in magazines. With the popularity of paperback books, fewer magazines were published and more stories became full length novels or collections of stories. These types of books also are called category fiction and are frequently shelved in labeled sections of the bookstore. As in the case of Bradbury, many authors have elevated category fiction to literary fiction.

Bradbury's best-known novel, *Fahrenheit 451* tells a story set in the future about a man named Montag who works as a "fireman"—a job title the society gives to workers who are assigned to burn books, which the **totalitarian** government has outlawed because of the supposedly dangerous ideas they contain. Montag meets a young girl who tells him about a time when books were legal and daily life was less restricted. Out of curiosity he begins stealing the books he is supposed to burn and becomes marked as a criminal who has to run for his life. The novel was made into a successful and haunting **film** by François Truffaut in 1966.

p.521

p.93

The Martian Chronicles is a collection of closely related stories detailing the adventures of space explorers when Earth colonizes the planet Mars and the Martians fight back in an attempt to prevent the destruction of their way of life. The colonists then face a tragedy of their own as a devastating nuclear war takes place on their home planet.

One of Bradbury's most autobiographical novels, *Dandelion Wine*, describes a landmark, surreal summer experienced by twelve-year-old Douglas Spaulding in the imaginary village of Greentown. Exploring the town with ambitious plans, Spaulding discovers the magic and mystery of a so-called "ordinary" landscape. *Dandelion Wine* later brought Bradbury his most unusual honor when Apollo astronauts named a depression on the moon Dandelion Crater, after Bradbury's book.

Something Wicked This Way Comes takes its title from a line spoken by a witch in William Shakespeare's dark drama *Macbeth* (pr. 1606). When a mysterious carnival comes to a small midwestern town, two thirteen-year-old boys are the only people who realize the evil effects the carnival is having on their fellow townspeople. The boys battle against disbelieving parents and authorities to expose the destructive agenda of the carnival's owner, appropriately named Mr. Dark.

– Carroll Dale Short

Fahrenheit 451, the Movie

Ray Bradbury's *Fahrenheit 451* was adapted to the screen by French director François Truffaut and released in 1966. Ray Bradbury has commented in interviews that he thought it was a good adaptation of his novel, and he was pleased with the casting of Oskar Werner in the role of Montag. The film depicts a future that shares much in common with our present. Montag commutes on a monorail from his home in a suburb of identical houses, much like the housing tracts of the American suburbs. His wife Linda constantly watches a big-screen TV and pops tranquilizers. It is interesting to both read the book and watch the movie. Viewers will be convinced about the value of reading and freedom of expression.

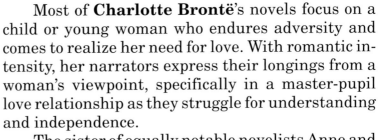

Charlotte Brontë

Born: April 21, 1816; Thornton, Yorkshire, England
Died: March 31, 1855; Haworth, Yorkshire, England

www.bronte.org.uk

TITLES

Jane Eyre, 1847

Shirley, 1849

Villette, 1853

The Professor, 1857

Emma, 1860 (fragment published in *Cornhill Magazine*)

Most of **Charlotte Brontë**'s novels focus on a child or young woman who endures adversity and comes to realize her need for love. With romantic intensity, her narrators express their longings from a woman's viewpoint, specifically in a master-pupil love relationship as they struggle for understanding and independence.

The sister of equally notable novelists Anne and Emily Brontë, Charlotte grew up in Haworth, a bleak village in Yorkshire surrounded by moors. Her p.95 father was the rector of the local Anglican church. After her mother died, she and her close-knit siblings read books and roamed the moors. When the family's two oldest girls were sent to school in Lancashire, Charlotte and Emily joined them in a school whose harshness Charlotte later immortalized in the fictional Lowood of *Jane Eyre*. Soon, the two elder sisters became ill and were brought home to die, an extremely distressing event for Charlotte and her brother.

Over the next five years, Charlotte and her remaining siblings learned and played at home, writing complex sagas of the imaginary kingdom of Angria in tiny books. Describing at length its wars, politics, aristocracy, loves, and feuds, Char-

Haworth

Haworth is the center of "Brontë Country." It is located in an area of moors and heather. The ground is made up mostly of a dark, craggy sandstone, which gives the landscape a bleak, desolate appearance. This is the landscape so common in the Brontës' novels. Sites in the area served as models for locations in their works and have become tourist attractions. Some forty miles away in the village of Cowan Bridge is the local school, which served as the inspiration for "Lowood School" in *Jane Eyre*. The Haworth parsonage, where the family lived, is now the Brontë Parsonage Museum.

lotte and her sisters occupied themselves with these enormously detailed narratives until they were in their twenties. Out of the remarkable stories of this kingdom came characters created by Charlotte who grappled with their own feelings in their search for passion, equality, and independence in love relationships. These stories also became a source of guilt for Charlotte because they depicted women whose feelings conflicted with the social ideals of her time.

Charlotte drew on her own experiences as a **governess** to write her first book, *The Professor*, which, through a role reversal, placed her own thoughts and feelings in the voice of a male tutor. In her next book, *Jane Eyre*, she used the main character's voice, introducing the most striking aspect of her novel—the use of a frank, intimate voice that conveys to the reader the speaker's emotional intensity in progressing from youthful rebellion to mature understanding.

Jane Eyre is an orphan who has suffered many difficulties and who proudly achieves self-discipline in the oppressive conditions at Lowood School. She accepts a position as governess at the home of Mr.

p.96

Governess

A governess is a woman who is hired by a family to care for the children. This is not a babysitter or nanny. The governess traditionally also was responsible for the child's education and social training. One example of a governess in literature and film is the character of Anna in *Anna and the King of Siam*, which became the musical and film *The King and I*.

Rochester and finds herself drawn to him. They plan to marry, but the revelation of his terrible secret causes their marriage plans to break down, and Jane leaves. Years later, after hardships and illness, Jane, a mature women returns to the home of Rochester, who is now blinded and maimed, and they begin their life together.

Charlotte Brontë wrote *Shirley* in 1849 and *Villette* in 1853, both books concerning women who fall in love and come to terms with the conflicts in their lives. Her final work, *Emma*, was unfinished.

Charlotte Brontë's strengths lie in her ability to tell a story through the sensibility of a child or a young woman, and her depiction of love from a woman's viewpoint.

– Mary Hurd

Emily Brontë

Born: July 30, 1818; Thornton, Yorkshire, England
Died: December 19, 1848; Haworth, Yorkshire, England

www.bronte.org.uk

Wuthering Heights, 1847

Next to playwright William Shakespeare's *Romeo and Juliet* (pr. 1595-1596), **Emily Brontë**'s *Wuthering Heights* is perhaps the best-known love story ever written. Full of violence, cruelty, terror, and death, it tells the story of Catherine and Heathcliff, whose powerful but frustrated love plays out against the background of the wild Yorkshire moors and turns into a powerful tale of revenge.

p.95

Emily Brontë spent almost her entire life in the Yorkshire village of **Haworth**, in the house of her father, the local parson. Few details of her private life have survived, but she seems to have been a recluse, preferring to spend most of her time roaming the moors with her pet hawk and her fierce dog or writing mystical poetry inspired by the dark and stormy Yorkshire landscape. She never married and seems not to have had any romances. The person to whom she may have been closest was her brother Branwell, who led an anguished life full of drink and disappointment; he may have been the model for Hindley, the angry brother of Catherine in *Wuthering Heights*. Emily was also close to two of her sisters, Anne and Charlotte, who also became novelists. In childhood, Emily and Anne invented the fantasy world of Gondal, about

which they wrote poems depicting murders, dungeons, and betrayals in love. In adulthood, Charlotte discovered Emily's poems and encouraged her to publish them, which she reluctantly did in 1846 in a book containing poems by all three sisters. A year later, the three sisters all published novels that would become famous: Charlotte's *Jane Eyre*, Anne's *The Tenant of Wildfell Hall*, and Emily's *Wuthering Heights*.

Like Brontë's poems about Gondal, *Wuthering Heights* combines an evocation of turbulent nature with a sense of mysticism and dark fantasy. In some ways, the novel is reminiscent of the gothic horror stories of the eighteenth century, complete with storms and a frightening old servant who continually mutters curses. It tells the story of the passionate love of Catherine, the daughter of the master of the Wuthering Heights estate, for the orphan Heathcliff. Catherine is drawn to the half savage Heathcliff, seeing him as her soul mate; however, she decides that she cannot marry him and instead weds Edgar Linton, the pleasant and rich heir to the neighboring estate, Thrushcross Grange. Rejected, Heathcliff flees, only to return years later to seek his revenge.

p.87 p.560

Consumption

Consumption, now known as tuberculosis, is a bacterial disease that most frequently attacks the lungs. It is quite common in developing countries, but modern medicines have helped to control its the spread in the developed world. During the nineteenth century, tuberculosis was widespread in Europe. The symptoms were not associated with a disease but rather signs of a sensitive personality, an artist, musician, poet, or writer. In 1880 Robert Koch discovered the cause of tuberculosis and medical scientists then began to look for ways to cure or control the disease.

Wuthering Heights, the Movies

Wuthering Heights has been adapted for the screen on many occasions, first in 1920 as a silent film, in 1939 in the best-known version, in 1970, again in 1992, and as a Masterpiece Theater series for television in 1998. The romantic story of mismatched lovers destined to be together in death lends itself to filmmaking on a grand scale. The 1939 version was a memorable film produced by Sam Goldwyn, directed by William Wyler, and starring Laurence Olivier as Heathcliff and Merle Oberon as Cathy. The English moors were recreated in California, with 450 acres of land completely relandscaped. Gregg Toland's moody black and white cinematography captured the atmosphere of the story and won him an Academy Award.

p.98

.99

At first regarded as brutal and strange, *Wuthering Heights* began to win praise after Brontë's early death of **consumption** for its power, passion, and intricate structure. It has been interpreted in various ways and has also been adapted many times for television and film, including a silent film version in 1920 and a popular film version starring Laurence Olivier in 1939.

– Sheldon Goldfarb

Bruce Brooks

Born: September 23, 1950; Washington, D.C.

www.scils.rutgers.edu/~kvander/brooks.html

p.233

Bruce Brooks places the young characters in his books in situations that try their ingenuity and reveal their toughness, intelligence, and coping skills. His believable **protagonists**, both male and female, suffer pain with grace and overcome hardships with ingenuity and imagination. He is primarily interested in how the hearts of young people work, how families fall apart and reunite, and how sports bond people together.

When Brooks was six years old, his parents divorced. Afterward he split his time between his father, who lived in urban Washington, and his mother and stepfather, who lived in rural North Carolina. Well before his teenage years, Brooks began writing, beginning with comic books then changing to prose exclusively. After finishing high school, he earned a bachelor's degree at the **University of North Carolina at Chapel Hill** and a master's degree at the p.194 University of Iowa. In time, he would develop a wide range of interests, including music, sports, and birds.

In Brooks's first novel, *The Moves Make the Man*, a black basketball player helps a white friend learn the game well enough to win an important wager. The protagonist of *Throwing Smoke* creates champion players on baseball cards who miraculously come alive and turn his losing team into a winning one. The Wolfbay Wings series follows the fortunes of young ice hockey players in their efforts to become winners.

Reflecting Brooks's interest in music and dysfunctional families, *Midnight Hour Encores* follows a teenage musical prodigy on a journey with her father to see her mother, who abandoned her as a child. *No Kidding* tells the story of a fourteen-year-old who looks after a younger brother because his father has joined a religious group and his mother has been institutionalized for alcoholism. In *Vanishing* an eleven-year-old girl is hospitalized for bronchitis, brought on by parental neglect. She doubts life is worth the struggle, but a fellow patient helps restore her faith in living. *Dolores* follows a young girl from

p.101

Alcoholism

Alcoholism is the physical dependence on alcoholic beverages and the problems in behavior and health that result from that dependence. Changes in behavior are noticable the more a person drinks, ranging from chattiness, to confusion, to unconsciousness, to death. While the scientific cause of why one person becomes an alcholic and another does not is not fully understood, programs using biological, psychological, and social approaches appear to help control alcoholic behavior. Of the programs used to help control alcoholism, the best known is Alcoholics Anonymous. Through education, meetings, and support of other members, Alcoholics Anonymous attempts to help alcoholics stop drinking forever.

Newbery Medal and Honor Books

The American Library Association, Childrens's Library Section, is responsible for selecting the Newbery Medal winner each year. Given since 1922 to the most distinguished American children's book published the previous year, the medal is named for the eighteenth century English bookseller John Newbery. The purpose is to give the same recognition to books for children that is given to poetry, plays, or novels for adults. It is the oldest and best known award given to the author of a children's book in the U.S.A. In addition to the award winner, the selection committee names Newbery Honor Books.

the age of seven to her teens as she experiences a foiled kidnapping and a near rape. *What Hearts* tells the story of a seven-year-old and his mother as they make a new life for themselves after trying to live with his stepfather. In *Asylum for Nightface*, a fourteen-year-old's wealthy parents join a cult and declare him a saint, setting the boy off in search of acceptance and love. *Everywhere* teaches the narrator the healing power of love when his grandfather suffers a heart attack.

Bruce Brooks's many writing awards include Newbery Honor Book recognition for *The Moves Make the Man* and *What Hearts*. *Everywhere* was named a Golden Kite Honor Book, and he received three *School Library Journal* **Best Book of the Year** citations.

p.102

p.195

p.111

– Bernard E. Morris

Terry Brooks

Born: January 8, 1944; Sterling, Illinois

www.terrybrooks.net

p.87

Terry Brooks has written three series of **fantasy** novels that appeal not only to young adult readers but also to older readers. His books are filled with creatures from mythology and legend. Several of his characters are young adults who face crises that force them to grow up quickly. He is best known 384 for his **best-selling** *Shannara* novels.

Brooks was born and reared in a tiny town in northwestern Illinois. He earned his bachelor's degree from Hamilton College in New York, where he majored in English literature and discovered the 104 works of **J. R. R. Tolkien**. He then earned a law degree at Washington and Lee University in Virginia. He began writing when he was ten years old, but his first novel, *The Sword of Shannara*, was not published until he was over thirty. He attempted several genres, including science fiction, war stories, and westerns, until he settled on writing fantasy. It took him seven years to write *The Sword of Shannara*, which became a best-seller. He practiced law in Sterling until 1986, when he became a full-time writer and moved to Seattle, Washington, with his wife Judine.

Brooks's *Shannara* stories are filled with elves, dwarves, gnomes, trolls, druids, warlocks, and magical swords. The early books in the series especially show Tolkien's influence and feature young adult characters. For example, Flick Ohmsford and his adoptive brother Shea of *The Sword of Shannara* are still living at home and working for their innkeeper father when they become embroiled in the

TITLES

Shannara novels:

The Sword of Shannara, 1977

The Elfstones of Shannara, 1982

The Wishsong of Shannara, 1985

The Scions of Shannara, 1990

The Druid of Shannara, 1991

The Elf Queen of Shannara, 1992

The Talismans of Shannara, 1993

The First King of Shannara, 1996

Ilse Witch, 2000

Antrax, 2001

Morgawr, 2002

Jarka Ruus, 2003

Tanequil, 2004

The Magic Kingdom of Landover novels:

Magic Kingdom for Sale—Sold!, 1986

The Black Unicorn, 1987

Wizard at Large, 1988

The Tangle Box, 1994

Witches Brew, 1995

The World and the Void trilogy:

Running with the Demon, 1997

A Knight of the Word, 1998

Angel Fire East, 1999

largest war their world has seen for two thousand years.

The *Landover* books, Brooks's second fantasy series, follow the adventures of Brooks's most autobiographical character, Ben Holiday, a lawyer living in Illinois. Holiday is about the same age that Brooks was when he wrote the first novel in the series. In *Magic Kingdom for Sale—Sold!*, Holiday, depressed over the death of his wife, responds to an advertisement offering a magical realm called Landover for sale. The ad is real, as Holiday discovers, but there is a catch.

Brooks's Word and Void books make up an urban fantasy series that is so dark that it might be classified as horror. It is set in the fictional city of Hopewell, which Brooks modeled on his hometown of

J. R. R. Tolkien

J. R. R. Tolkien was born in South Africa. When he was four years old, his father died, and his mother returned to England. The green English countryside made an impression on him, and it would become the setting for his now-famous fantasy world. In 1937, he published *The Hobbit,* a novel for children. It became an immediate success. Based on stories he made up for his children, it appealed to both young and old. Even more successful was *The Lord of the Rings,* a three-part work that described the fantastic world of Middle Earth. Tolkien fan clubs and magazines were founded, and he received awards and honors. With the release of Peter Jackson's blockbuster movie trilogy in 2001, 2002, and 2003, new fans discovered Tolkien's work.

Novelization

We are familiar with novels that are made into movies. A novelization is the reverse: a movie that is made into a novel. When a movie attracts a loyal audience, a writer may be commissioned to take the screenplay and construct a novel out of it. A screenplay relies on sets, actors, and filmed action to fill out a story. A novel requires that the writer suggest those viewed features to the reader. Novelizations generally are published as paperback novels and appeal to the fans of the movie.

Sterling. He kept the real name for Sinissippi Park, which is a center for supernatural activity in the area. One of the main characters is Nest Freemark, a fourteen-year-old girl at the beginning of *Running with the Demon*, the first book in the series. Although she has magical powers, she must still cope with the pains of adolescence, the suicide of her mother, the disappearance of her father, and the alcoholism of her grandmother.

p.101

In addition to his original fiction, Terry Brooks has written two movie novelizations, *Hook* (1991) and *Stars Wars: Episode One: The Phantom Menace* p.105 (1999). He frequently appears at fantasy conventions, book festivals, writer's conferences, and book-signing parties at bookstores.

– Thomas R. Feller

Ashley Bryan

Born: July 13, 1923; New York, New York

www.cbcbooks.org/html/ashleybryan.html

Ashley Bryan is best known for compiling and retelling traditional African folk tales for young readers. His work, which is best appreciated when read aloud, explores the African American experience from the perspective of oral tradition and is dedicated to introducing traditional African stories to an American audience. Cultural themes play a large part in his work. He wants his readers to be rooted in their cultural traditions. He has been heavily influenced by African American poets, particularly Langston Hughes, p.107 and also has a great interest in African American spirituals, which he has collected in several books.

Bryan's parents were immigrants to the United States from the Caribbean island of Antigua, and he was born in New York and raised in the Bronx. Although he and his five siblings grew up in a tough neighborhood during the Depression years, they p.437 were avid readers who made good use of the public library. After graduating from high school, Bryan entered Cooper Union Art School, where he earned p.380 scholarships for his writing and illustrating. After serving in World War II, he earned a degree in philosophy from Columbia University and received a Fulbright Scholarship to study art in Europe. He p.80 later taught at Queen's College, Lafayette College,

Langston Hughes

Langston Hughes was a major influence on many twentieth century African American writers. He wrote novels, stories, and plays but is best known for his poetry. He is called the "The Poet Laureate of Black America" and was concerned for the ordinary African American and the paradox of being not quite free in a land of freedom. He also introduced African American patterns of speech into his poetry. The 1920's was a creative period in the African American community called the Harlem Renaissance, and Hughes was at the center of this creative movement, even incorporating elements of African American jazz music into his poetry.

and Dartmouth before leaving the academic life to pursue his writing.

Bryan began putting together his first books while he was in kindergarten and continued creating beautiful hand-made books for family and friends for years. During the 1960's a book editor admired one of Bryan's books and encouraged him to pursue a career as a children's **illustrator**. He then began illustrating, adapting, and writing books. His first book, *The Ox of the Wonderful Horns and Other African Folk Tales* is a collection of five African folk tales. *Beat the Story-Drum, Pum-Pum* retells five Nigerian folk tales in rhythmic language, illustrated with woodcuts. *The Cat's Purr* relates an amusing folk tale of how the cat got his purr, with fluid, sketchbook quality illustrations. p.38

The Story of Lightning and Thunder relates a Nigerian folk tale, explaining why thunder and lightning reside in the sky, rather than on earth. *Ashley Bryan's African Tales, Uh-Huh* is a collection of some of his favorite folk-tales, previously published in other books. *The Night Has Ears* is a collection of twenty-six African proverbs, both serious and humorous.

The May Hill Arbuthnot Honor Lecture Award

May Hill Arbuthnot was an important educator and writer of children's readers. She created and wrote the influential Curriculum Foundation Readers, best known as the "Dick and Jane" books, along with educator William Scott Gray. These books were published by the Scott, Foresman Company and were responsible for teaching generations of school children to read. They were published from 1930 to 1965. Interestingly, 1965 marked the year that the series introduced African American characters; it was also in that year that public schools began the process of racial integration across the nation.

A frequent public reader and lecturer, Arbuthnot was honored to have her name associated with an award given by the Association of Library Service to Children. Each year at the American Library Association midwinter meeting, an individual is named who will prepare a paper that contributes to the field of children's literature. Library schools, departments of education, or a children's library can apply to host the public reading of this paper. The award was started by publisher Scott, Foresman in 1969.

p.108
In 1990 Ashley Bryan received the **May Hill Arbuthnot Honor Lecture Award** for international achievement in children's literature. He also won the **Coretta Scott King Award** for *Beat the Story-Drum, Pum-Pum* and four of his books were selected as **Coretta Scott King Honor Books**. Bryan is much sought after as a speaker.

p.6

– Mary Virginia Davis

Eve Bunting

Born: December 19, 1928; Maghera, County Derry, Northern Ireland

www.kidsreads.com/authors/au-bunting-eve.asp

Eve Bunting has written more than 150 books, both fiction and nonfiction, but her favorite format is the picture book. She has also written for all age groups, from preschoolers to young adults, and is best known for her books dealing with topical and socially conscious themes, such as racial prejudice and **homelessness**. She is also the author of a series of horse stories under the pen name of Evelyn Bolton.

Born in Northern Ireland, Bunting studied at Queen's University in Belfast and grew up enjoying the Irish storytelling tradition. She also developed a social conscience and an awareness of prejudice at an early age from her experience of living in the troubled atmosphere of Northern Ireland. Partly to get away from the religious and political unrest there she moved to California with her husband and three children in 1958. As her children grew up, she searched for something to occupy her time and took a class in writing at a local community college. Although she was forty years old at the time, she had never before considered a career as a writer.

Bunting's best-known children's books tackle difficult topics. In *One More Flight* an eleven-year-old boy runs away from a center for emotionally disturbed children who are awaiting foster-home placement. He meets a man who rehabilitates injured eagles and hawks to return them to the

wild. *The Wall* describes the visit of a boy and his father to the **Vietnam Veterans Memorial** in Washington, D.C., where they find the name of the boy's grandfather inscribed on the wall. *Fly Away Home*, about a homeless boy and his father living in the airport, deftly handles this sensitive subject for young readers. *Smoky Night* concerns yet another serious issue, the Los Angeles riots of 1992, as seen through the eyes of a young boy from his window. With the help of his mother, he learns the importance of getting along with people no matter what their origins or ethnicity.

p.11

Bunting's young adult fiction also tackles controversial issues. In *If I Asked You, Would You Stay?* a seventeen-year-old boy's solitary existence is jeopardized when he rescues a troubled girl from the ocean and begins to fall in love with her. *A Sudden Silence* is the story of a boy's search for the **drunk driver** who killed his deaf brother in a hit-and-run accident. Remorseful that he could not save his brother, he also feels guilty that he is attracted to his dead brother's girlfriend. The novel deals with guilt, **alcoholism**, grief, and survival. *SOS Titanic* is a **historical novel** for young adults that tells the tale of an **upper-class** fifteen-year-old Irishman on a transatlantic journey to reunite

p.5
p.10
p.117
p.3

Vietnam Veterans Memorial

The Vietnam Veterans Memorial sits on a two-acre site at the foot of the Lincoln Memorial on the Mall in Washington, D.C. It honors the sacrifice of American military personnel during one of the nation's least popular wars. The memorial consists of three sections. The Wall, designed by Maya Lin, consists of a long, black granite wall on which are etched the names of 58,235 men and women who died or were missing in the Vietnam War. It was dedicated in 1982. The Wall was controversial because of its modern design. As a compromise, the Three Servicemen Statue and flagpole, designed by Frederick Hart, was added to the site in 1984. A third statue, the Vietnam Women's Memorial designed by Glenna Goodacre, was dedicated in 1993 to highlight the service of women in Vietnam.

The Golden Kite Award

The Golden Kite Award is to children's book authors and artists what an Academy Award is to professionals in the film industry: a reflection of recognition by their peers. Four Golden Kite statuettes are awarded each year, for fiction, non-fiction, picture book text, and picture book illustration. The winning author or illustrator must be a member of the Society of Chldren's Book Writers and Illustrators. The works chosen are those that the judges feel exhibit excellence and appeal to the interests and concerns of children.

with his parents. Along the way he begins to learn about class injustice, has experiences with the supernatural, and finds romance.

Eve Bunting received a Golden Kite Award for *One More Flight* and a **Southern California Council on Literature Award for Fiction** for the *Ghost of Summer*. The American Library Association also honored *If I Asked You, Would You Stay?* as one of the **Best Books for Young Adults** of 1984, and Bunting received the 1984 PEN **Special Achievement Award** for contributions to children's literature.

— Mary Virginia Davis

11

480

p.45

p.723

Frances Hodgson Burnett

Born: November 24, 1849; Manchester, England
Died: October 29, 1924; Plandome, New York

www.literature-web.net/burnett

Frances Hodgson Burnett's books for children attract readers of all ages. Set in nineteenth century England, with scenes in India and America, her novels evoke a variety of Victorian landscapes, homes, and character types, and offer insights into the minds of her young characters, hints of myth and magic, and delightful plots and plot reversals.

Born Frances Eliza Hodgson, Burnett grew up in the industrial city of Manchester in central En-

gland. When her father died in 1854, her mother took over the family foundry, but the business failed because of blockades set up during the United States Civil War. In 1865 the family moved to a log cabin in Tennessee. Burnett began writing when she was nineteen and sold her first story to the popular magazine *Godey's Lady's Book*. Soon she was regularly selling stories about life in England to American magazines, and her family prospered. In 1873 she married Dr. Swan Burnett, whom she later divorced. The couple had two sons.

Burnett's books reflect her own childhood uprooting and financial reversals. In *Little Lord Fauntleroy*, her most famous book, an American boy learns that he is the grandson of a wealthy English earl and only a week later finds himself standing in front of an English castle. This popular novel was embraced by mothers on both continents who were charmed by young Cedric **Fauntleroy's** long curls, velvet suit, and lace collar (which Burnett modeled after playwright Oscar Wilde). They also loved his kind heart because he wants to give his newly acquired riches to poor children.

Sara Crewe is an irresistible riches-to-rags-and-back story. Sara, a young girl from India attending a London **boarding school**, learns that her adored father has died in financial ruin. The nasty Miss Minchin, her school's headmistress, moves Sara to a drafty attic and makes her work as a servant, casting Sara into even deeper despair. However, she is strong, despite her pampered upbringing, and bears her misfortunes bravely. In a surprise turn, a mysterious gentleman from India arrives with his servant, Ram Dass, and they work magic in Sara's life. In 1905 Burnett rewrote the story as a play, then expanded the original novel, titling both versions *A Little Princess*.

In 1909 Burnett moved to a house in **Long Island**, New York. Soon afterward, work began on a hidden walled garden, which inspired her to write a novel called

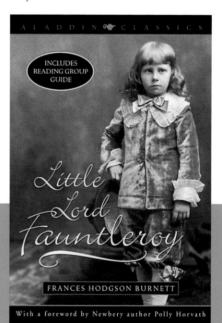

Little Lord Fauntleroy

The character of Little Lord Fauntleroy has long gone beyond the pages of the book of the same name. The style of clothing described by Burnett in the book was embraced by mothers in the late 1800's and early 1900's for their young sons. Boys from the age of five up to the age of thirteen were often dressed by their mothers in black or dark blue velvet suits, with short knee-length pants and white lace-trimmed shirts. They wore either black or white knee length stockings. They often had long curly hair topped by a hat. The term, a "Little Lord Fauntleroy," has come to suggest a pampered, prissy boy.

FRANCES HODGSON BURNETT

The Secret Garden. The story begins in India with the spoiled, foot-stomping Mary Lennox, a child ignored by her parents and indulged by servants. Orphaned during a cholera outbreak, Mary is sent to live with a depressed uncle in a mansion on the lonely moors of England. Her new servant, Martha, decides it is time for Mary to learn to do things for herself. In one of the most powerful character transformations in children's literature, the helpless Mary is soon dressing herself, playing outside, skipping rope, and best of all, tending a secret garden with a wild mythic boy from the moors and an invalid cousin from the mansion.

Frances Burnett also wrote more than forty novels for adults, several plays, and a memoir of her childhood. Her children's books have all been dramatized as plays or **films**.

– Jan Allister

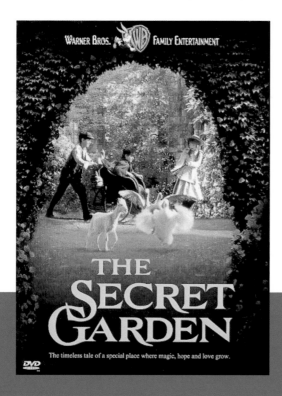

The Secret Garden, the Movies

The Secret Garden was first adapted to the big screen in 1949 and then again in 1993. While the story may seem somewhat old-fashioned for modern viewers, these films enchant the viewer by bringing to life the setting, characters, and themes in Burnett's beloved novel. Presenting topics not always familiar in children's films—Mary's parents die, she discovers her invalid cousin hidden away in a spooky manor, a harsh governess takes no responsibility for her charge—the movies portray them in a believable way and put across the message of renewal through friendship and caring without being too sugary.

Hester Burton

Born: December 6, 1913; Beccles, Suffolk, England
Died: 2003

www.collectingbooksandmagazines.com/
hesterburton.html

The **protagonists** of **Hester Burton**'s many **historical novels** are young adults who live in exciting but dangerous times. As great events swirl around them, they discover their own capacities for heroism, especially in battles against social injustice.

Hester Burton was born Hester Wood-Hill in Beccles, Suffolk, England. Her mother read classic novels to her and her older sisters. Her father, a family doctor, was the model for several wise, idealistic characters in her books. When she was six, Burton had a series of illnesses that kept her confined to her bed, where she entertained herself by inventing plots for her toy soldiers. At twelve, she was sent to Headington School in Oxford. There, because she was too delicate for sports, she spent her spare time reading historical novels.

Burton completed her education at **Oxford University**, where in 1936 she received an honors degree in English literature. The following year, she married Reginald W. B. Burton, an Oxford tutor and lecturer. During the early years of their marriage, the couple hosted families who had lost their homes when the **Germans attacked London** during World War II. Burton saw in these dark times parallels with her favorite historical period, the early nine-

233
117
173
p.41

Napoleon I

Napoleon Bonaparte was a military leader who benefited politically from the French Revolution. By 1804, he had declared himself emperor of France. England, Austria, Russia, and Sweden formed an alliance against him, but he defeated their armies at Austerlitz in 1805. By 1808, he was master of the European continent. Only the sea power of England kept him from creating an empire. In today's language, Napoleon was a "control freak." He refused to delegate authority to others and attempted to control both military and government matters himself. Between 1808 and 1814, Napoleon continued to succeed in war, but he drove his troops too hard. In 1812, he advanced on the Russian city of Moscow, with 500,000 troops. With winter approaching, the Russians struck back and drove Napoleon's troops back to Paris. When Paris fell in 1814, Napolen stepped down from power and was exiled to the island of Elba. He attempted to rally the French troops one more time but was defeated at the Battle of Waterloo in 1815. He lived the rest of his life in exile on the island of Saint Helena.

teenth century, when her nation feared an invasion by another dictator, the French emperor **Napoleon**.

After her youngest daughter entered nursery school in 1949, Burton began teaching part time. That same year she also published her first book, a biography of a nineteenth century British feminist. Soon afterward, Burton began editing nonfiction works for young adults. It then occurred to her that she would enjoy writing fiction for that same audience. Her first book, *The Great Gale* (1960), later republished as *The Flood at Reedsmore* (1968), dealt with a recent event. Her second book, *Casters Away!* (1962), which takes place at the time of the Battle of Trafalgar in 1805, was her first true historical novel.

Burton's best-known novel, *Time of Trial*, is also set early in the nineteenth century. Its narrator is seventeen-year-old Margaret Pargeter, the daughter of a London bookseller. Her father's defiant publications attacking slum-lords and child labor bring him to the verge of ruin. He is sent to prison for sedition, and his bookshop is burned by a mob. Meanwhile, Margaret falls in love with a young **medical student**, whose wealthy family disapproves of their union. Eventually they marry, and Margaret's father emerges from prison, planning to rebuild his bookshop and to continue crusading.

Hester Burton has been commended for the fact that although she hopes to develop the social conscience of her audience, her books are not dully moralistic. They owe their popularity to the fact that her characters are well developed, her plots riveting, and her settings presented in such authentic detail that readers feel as if they have been transported to other times and places. Burton's books have won critical acclaim and numerous honors, including Britain's **Carnegie Medal** for *Time of Trial* and a **Boston Globe-Horn Honor Book** award for *Beyond the Weir Bridge*.

– Rosemary M. Canfield Reisman

PENGUIN CLASSICS

CHARLES DICKENS
A Tale of Two Cities

Historical Fiction

Works of historical fiction are set in a real setting from history with fictional characters. Many of the background events may have really happened, but the characters are imagined by the author, and likewise their actions and comments come from the author's imagination. Charles Dickens' *A Tale of Two Cities* is a work of historical fiction. While placing the action in France and England during the French Revolution reflects actual events, Dickens portrays fictional characters who reflect his own views of human values and human nature.

Aidan Chambers

Born: December 27, 1934; Chester-le-Street, County
Durham, England

aidanchambers.co.uk

Aidan Chambers is an advocate of children's and young adult literature. While many of his most noted works are young adult novels, he also has written books for readers of all ages and produced a body of drama, nonfiction, criticism, and anthologies on such subjects as ghosts and science fiction. He maintains that children and young adults ought to be encouraged to read things that interest them, and that adults should take a supportive and nonjudgmental role in their children's reading choices.

An only child whose earliest years were spent in a rural environment, Chambers had few friends and relied on his own imagination to amuse himself. Early in his school career, he was a reluctant student plagued by poor teachers. School was more tolerable after he learned to read well enough to do so voraciously. By the age of fifteen, he wished to become an author. He was not able to pursue this ambition immediately, however. After finishing school and serving in the military for two years, he attended college and became an English teacher. He then decided to become a monk and spent seven years in a Roman Catholic monastery before returning to teaching and

writing. In 1960 he married. With his wife's encouragement, he left teaching to write full time and edit the journal *Signal*.

p.119

Chambers's recurring themes in his books are fidelity, bravery, and honesty with one's self. Questions about their sexuality often propel his characters to self-knowledge and something approaching wisdom. His books have been praised for their honest portrayals of adolescent emotions and complicated lives. *Dance on My Grave* deals sympathetically, and with complexity, with the emotional turmoil of a young man named Hal after the death of a friend named Barry with whom he has had a p.57 homosexual relationship. Barry's mother blames him for her son's death, and much of the novel is spent sorting out conflicting information to get at the truth of the boys' relationship, as well as the meaning of an apparently vicious action that Hal undertakes at Barry's grave.

In *The Toll Bridge*, unhappy seventeen-year-old Jan takes a job as a toll-bridge collector and befriends Adam and Tess. In the course of their friendship, each of the three is faced with important, life-changing decisions, as well as with revelations about their characters and their priorities.

Chambers's later novel *Postcards from No Man's Land* is an ambitious and successful supernatural love story. It is set during World War II and in the mid-1990's. During the war, a young Dutch woman named Geertrui falls in love with a wounded

Signal

The Thimble Press was founded by Aidan Chambers and his American-born wife Nancy Lockwood in 1969 to publish the journal *Signal: Approaches to Children's Books*. The journal, edited by Lockwood, was published three times a year and collected articles on children's literature and education. The highly respected journal stopped publication in 2003.

Hans Christian Andersen Award

The Hans Christian Andersen Award has been presented every other year since 1956 by the International Board on Books for Young People (IBBY). The IBBY was founded in 1953 and there are branches in countries around the world. The award is presented to one author and one illustrator for his or her body of work. It is often called the "little Nobel," referring to the Nobel Prize for Literature. The award winner receives a gold medal and a diploma.

British soldier whom she hides from the Nazis. In the late 1990's, seventeen-year old Jacob, the grandson of a British soldier who died in World War II, goes to Amsterdam to commemorate his grandfather's sacrifice. There he meets an elderly woman, who serves as the second narrator of the novel. This book, which won an **American Library Association Best Books for Young Adults** award, deals with issues of sexuality, heroism, and fidelity. In 2002, Chambers was honored with the **Hans Christian Andersen Award** for his body of work.

– Angela M. Salas

p.45
p.480
p.120

Alice Childress

Born: October 12, 1916; Charleston, South Carolina
Died: August 4, 1994; Queens, New York

www.scils.rutgers.edu/~cybers/childress2.html

A playwright, director, producer, and actor with the American Negro Theater during the 1940's and 1950's, **Alice Childress** was the first African American woman to earn an **Obie Award** for best Off-Broadway play for *Trouble in Mind* (pr. 1956). With the publication of *A Hero Ain't Nothin' but a Sandwich* in 1973, Childress began a long and distinguished career as a young adult author. Like her early drama, her young adult fiction addresses the complexities of racial and gender prejudice, particularly for young African Americans who, in her view, were often overlooked by mainstream media.

Childress was born in Charleston, South Carolina. When she was five, she moved to **Harlem** in p.296 New York City to live with her grandmother, Eliza Campbell, who helped nurture her early creative aspirations. In her grandmother's church, Childress learned about the social and racial struggles with which African Americans, particularly women, were forced to contend.

A Hero Ain't Nothin' but a Sandwich, Childress's first novel, earned a **National Book Award** nomination for its forthright

.122

TITLES

A Hero Ain't Nothin' but a Sandwich, 1973

Rainbow Jordan, 1981

Those Other People, 1989

look at the issue of teenage drug addiction. Set during the 1960's, the novel depicts the life of a young heroin addict, Benjie Johnson, and includes the perspectives of the people around him who shape his immediate environment, including family, friends, and even the pusher who supplies his drugs. Childress links Benjie's decline as a junkie to a variety of sources, such as family strife, peer pressure, and a pervasive climate of racial prejudice, all of which contribute to Benjie's increasing alienation and despair. Though highly acclaimed by critics, the novel p.74 was **banned** in some schools and libraries for nearly a decade because of what was perceived as controversial subject matter.

In *Rainbow Jordan*, a teenage girl confronts her unhappy past with the help of a foster parent. Born to teenage parents and abandoned at an early age by her father, Rainbow Jordan grows up seeking the love and attention of her resentful and sometimes physically abusive mother, Katherine Jordan. At the age of five, Rainbow is discovered alone in her burning apartment by firefighters, and she begins a long journey through

National Book Award

The National Book Award was started in 1950 by a number of book publishing groups united in the quest to enhance the public awareness of outstanding books and to increase the popularity of reading. Since that time it has become one of the most important literary awards in the U.S. Nominated books are evaluated by a committee and winners are selected in the categories of fiction, nonfiction, poetry, and young people's literature. The winners each receive $10,000 plus a crystal trophy.

Foster Care

State or county governments oversee child welfare agencies that look out for neglected or abused children. When a child's family is unable to provide care, the child may be placed in a foster home. Once a family has been screened and approved for foster care, a child may join that family. A social worker will be assigned to monitor the care of that child in the home. Some foster home relationships last a long time, and others only a short time. It is often difficult for the child placed in foster care to feel a sense of family or of belonging. This often leads to problem behavior and poor performance in school.

23
numerous foster homes. Nine years later, Rainbow's social worker finds her a home with Josephine Lamont, a woman in her forties who has recently been deserted by her husband. The novel chronicles the nurturing relationship that forms between Rainbow and Josephine as they help each other adjust to the changing circumstances of their lives.

In *Those Other People*, Childress addresses the issues of racism, homophobia, and sexual abuse. p.263 Seventeen-year-old Jonathon, who is struggling with his own sexuality and his plans for the future, decides to become a high school computer instructor instead of enrolling in college. He soon becomes embroiled in controversy as some of his students object 401 to the school's desegregation and his homosexuality. p.57 When a young student accuses a fellow teacher of sexual abuse, Jonathon is compelled to face the abuse of his peers and the community at large in order to discover the truth about the alleged sexual abuse.

– Philip Bader

Kate Chopin

Born: February 8, 1851; St. Louis, Missouri
Died: August 22, 1904; St. Louis, Missouri

www.teenreads.com/authors/au-chopin-kate.asp

TITLES

The Awakening, 1899

A Vocation and a Voice, 1991

The nineteenth century female characters who populate **Kate Chopin**'s works explore their increasing desires for personal fulfillment, often in regard to love, and resent the society that inhibits them. Frequently confined to traditional roles by their husbands and other family members, these women struggle to free themselves. In spite of having seemingly secure lives, they yearn for release from meaningless social activities and male domination.

Chopin was born Katherine O'Flaherty in St. Louis, Missouri, where she grew up. She had mixed Creole and Irish ancestry. After her p.125 father died in a train wreck, leadership of the family fell to her maternal great-grandmother, who provided for her education. The personal experiences she had while growing up supplied the necessary background and expertise required for her remarkable emergence as a seminal American author. St. Louis was a comparatively cosmopolitan city, and Chopin became proficient in French and German. She was also well read in contemporary European literature and was a successful pianist. After marrying Oscar Chopin, she traveled in Europe and then settled in New Orleans, where she enjoyed the tolerant nature of Creole society. She became a writer only af-

ter her husband's death—as a way of supporting herself and her six children.

126
The success of Chopin's **local-color** stories in magazines encouraged her to try writing novels. In 1899, she published *The Awakening*, her second attempt at a novel, with high expectations. Although the work was eventually considered a masterpiece, it shocked contemporary readers. The protagonist p.233 of the novel, Edna Pontellier, was deemed immoral and the theme of the book coarse and degrading. Edna is a young wife and the mother of two children, living in New Orleans and vacationing at nearby Grande Isle. After she "awakens" to her combined needs for sexual and artistic fulfillment, she eventually abandons her family. Tragically, she recognizes that her identity as a mother is inescapable and that this responsibility is irreconcilable with her newly achieved self-awareness.

Late nineteenth century readers were offended by the idea of a woman's flouting traditional boundaries merely to satisfy a sense of personal fulfillment. Chopin's earlier stories had not prepared the public for her newly forthright treatment of human

Creole

Creole has been used to identify different groups of people at different times. It has identified native peoples of the West Indies or Central and South America. It later referred to children born in the Americas of Spanish, then French parents, a designation that applied to Chopin's mother's family. It also has been used to identify residents of Louisiana or the Caribbean who were not native, such as Europeans or Africans. After the Louisiana Purchase, residents of Louisiana who were of European ancestry called themselves Creole and restricted slaves and free blacks from identifying themselves as such. After the Civil War, people in Louisiana of mixed ancestry, usually European and African, again began to be identified as Creoles. The term also applies to their music and cooking.

Local-Color Writing

Local-color writing refers to stories or novels in which the geographical setting plays an important role. Writers such as Bret Harte and Mark Twain used the American West to create a special atmosphere for many of their works. Sarah Orne Jewett created characters tied to the world of New England. The Creole culture of New Orleans and the Southern plantations were crucial to the writing of George Washington Cable. Being an outsider in rural Louisiana, Kate Chopin was able to observe life in this unique environment and tie character and place together in her stories.

sexuality. Publication of a collection of her short stories was cancelled and her career as a writer came to an abrupt end.

Kate Chopin's story collection, *A Vocation and a Voice*, was not published until 1991—long after the rare achievement of *The Awakening* had been fully realized. Many of the stories rise above the local color designation. Especially appealing is "The Story of an Hour," in which the report of a husband's untimely death unexpectedly results in his wife's eager anticipation of freedom from marital bonds. Although the themes, characters and events in Chopin's works no longer scandalize readers, her vivid portrayals of women in transition add validity and depth to the literature of the era and to American literature as a whole.

— Margaret A. Dodson

Agatha Christie

Born: September 15, 1890; Torquay, England
Died: January 12, 1976; Wallingford, England
www.agathachristie.com

Agatha Christie was one of the most prolific and popular mystery writers of the twentieth century. No matter whom Christie used as her investigator, her mysteries consistently present murders as puzzles that can be solved by observation of people's behavior and conversation rather than through abstract science or encyclopedic knowledge of things such as train time tables. Christie's villains are never easy to pin down, either—anyone may be a murderer: a businessman, a scheming wife, an apparently brainless blonde, a schoolgirl, a shopkeeper, an aristocrat, or even the narrator of one of her novels.

Born Agatha Mary Clarissa Miller in southern England's seaside resort town of Torquay (the setting of a popular British television show, *Fawlty Towers*). She had a wealthy American father and an English mother. Although her older sister attended an exclusive girls' school, Agatha herself was kept home to test her mother's belief that formal education was a bad thing for women. Agatha learned to read on her own and was writing stories and poems by the age of eleven. As a teenager she studied music in France but was too shy to pursue performing as a career. She returned to Torquay as World War I was starting and married a dashing pilot named Archibald Christie. While her husband fought in the war, she worked in a local hospital. At her sister's suggestion, she began thinking of a murder mystery plot, which eventually turned into her first novel, *The Mysterious Affair at Styles*.

TITLES

The Mysterious Affair at Styles, 1920

The Murder of Roger Ackroyd, 1926

The Murder at the Vicarage, 1930

Murder on the Orient Express, 1934 (publ. in the United States as *Murder on the Calais Coach*)

Death on the Nile, 1937

And Then There Were None, 1940

Evil Under the Sun, 1941

The Body in the Library, 1942

Mrs. McGinty's Dead, 1952

A Pocket Full of Rye, 1953

What Mrs. McGillicuddy Saw!, 1957

The Pale Horse, 1961

At Bertram's Hotel, 1965

By the Pricking of My Thumb, 1968

Nemesis, 1971

Elephants Can Remember, 1972

Curtain, 1975

Sleeping Murder, 1976

In 1926 Christie rocked the publishing world with her seventh novel, *The Murder of Roger Ackroyd*, which had a trick ending that caused a sensation. By then she was recognized as a leading mystery writer. Around that same time, however, she was having marital problems, and her husband wanted a divorce. One evening after an argument with her husband, she went to a resort town in northern England and checked into a hotel under the name of her husband's lover. **The disappearance** of a **best-selling** murder mystery writer sparked a nationwide hunt that increased her fame still more. She got her divorce in 1928 and married archaeologist Max Mallowan two years later. She accompanied her second husband on many of his digs in Syria and Iraq and set several of her mysteries in the same places.

p.384

p.1

Christie's two most popular detectives were the fussy and precise Belgian private detective Hercule Poirot, whom she introduced in her first novel, and the British Sleuth Miss Jane Marple, an apparently inconsequential old woman with a sharp eye for human nature and small-town life, whom she introduced in *The Murder at the Vicarage*. Poirot had been inspired by Belgian refugees quartered near Torquay during World War I. In one of Christie's

CLASSIC MYSTERY
AGATHA CHRISTIE COLLECTION
Dustin Hoffman   Vanessa Redgrave
Agatha
The mystery is factual.
The solution is ingenious.

Agatha, the Movie

In 1979, a fictional account of Christie's sensational eleven day disapperance was made into a movie starring Vanessa Redgrave as Agatha Christie. Dustin Hoffman plays an American journalist who searches for Christie and finds her in a spa. He uncovers her plan to commit suicide, making it look as if her husband's secretary and lover, who is also staying at the spa, killed her. In reality, Christie went into a tailspin over the collapse of her marriage. She did disappear for eleven days, and a costly search was conducted to find her. She turned up at a health spa unharmed and claiming she had no memory of what had gone on during that time.

The Mousetrap

Agatha Christie also wrote successful plays, one of which, *The Mousetrap*, has been performed on stage in London for fifty-one years, the longest-running legitamite play in history. The set for Christie's classic whodunit was pulled down in 1999 and auctioned for charity. The play continued performances at St. Martin's Theatre with a new set and continues to draw audiences. She also won an the New York Drama Critics Circle Award in 1953 for her play *Witness for the Prosecution*, which became a successful film in 1957.

later novels, her fictional mystery writer and alter ego, Ariadne Oliver, comments that if she had realized how long she would be writing about this character, she would not have given him so many quirks that had to be perpetuated from novel to novel.

Agatha Christie was named a Dame of the British Empire in 1971. Many of her novels have been made into movies, some several times. The 1945 version of *And Then There Were None* is a classic, as is the 1974 version of *Murder on the Orient Express*. A series of movies based on Miss Marple mysteries were made in the 1960's, and both Miss Marple and Hercule Poirot have become staples of a British television mystery series.

— Leslie Ellen Jones

Sandra Cisneros

Born: December 20, 1954; Chicago, Illinois

www.sandracisneros.com/home.html

p.233

The protagonists of **Sandra Cisneros**'s fiction tend to be young Latinas who are intelligent, brave, and sometimes introverted. The world in which they grow up is a bicultural, bilingual, occasionally hostile and economically depressed, but always fascinating environment. Whether located in Chicago, Illinois; San Antonio, Texas; or Mexico City, each of Cisneros's books draws its strength from a carefully described neighborhood that is explored through the bright eyes of an energetic young female narrator. The social relationships among Latino families, and the ever-present touch of some magic add excitement to Cisneros's work.

Cisneros was born the only daughter in a working-class family of seven children that lived in a dingy apartment on Chicago's tough South Side. Her father often took the family to Mexico to care for his mother. When Cisneros was fifteen, the family bought their first home. This childhood and teenage experience would provide the background of much of Cisneros's fiction. Her young characters have to survive in a tough world.

Cisneros began to publish after attending the University of Iowa Writers' Workshop when she was in her mid-twenties. She continued to write while teaching at universities.

p.131

The House on Mango Street is Cisneros's first and perhaps best known work. Its related short stories tell the experience of Esperanza, a young teenager growing up in a Latino neighborhood populated by her girlfriends, members of her family, and the well-observed inhabitants of the Latino community. An antique shop owned by an elderly African American holds as many mysteries as an abandoned junkyard. The smell of her family's food is as vividly described as the fates of some of her girlfriends.

Woman Hollering Creek is set in Texas and Mexico. Its female protagonists are Latina teenagers and young women who must make decisions in their private and family lives. Relationships with boyfriends, fathers, or lovers are always full of difficulties. Mothers and grandmothers offer help as young women pursue their own lives. They also must balance the charms and hardships of Mexican culture and address the demands of mainstream America. A hint of **Magical Realism** seeps into this book, which also features a witch.

Caramelo explores the coming of age of Celaya "Lala" Reyes. Like Cisneros's own family, the Reyes travel every year from Chicago to Mexico to visit the

University of Iowa Writers' Workshop

The University of Iowa Writers' Workshop was the first graduate program to accept a work of creative writing as a thesis for an advanced degree. It began in 1936, and is a two-year residency program that ends with the submission of a creative work—a novel, collection of poetry or short stories—and the awarding of a Master of Fine Arts degree. Young writers come to exchange ideas and creative suggestions. The Workshop has helped many well-known writers develop their writing skills, and attracts many famous writers as visiting faculty. While the program does not think that creative writing can be taught, it does believe that those with talent can be helped to develop that talent.

Before Columbus Foundation American Book Awards

The Before Columbus Foundation began giving the American Book Awards in 1978. Each year, at the annual American Booksellers Association convention, writers are honored for outstanding literary achievement. The selection of writers is made without restriction to race, sex, ethnic background, or genre in order to acknowledge the contribution to multicultural diversity and excellence in writing.

grandparents. As Lala grows up in the United States and Mexico, she keeps an eye open for adventures. Her "awful" Mexican grandmother has a striped shawl, called *caramelo rebozo*, that gives Lala a connection to her heritage. The quick, energetic dialogue captures the spirit of Spanish-English conversation, and Cisneros tells a magnificent story.

Sandra Cisneros's fiction gives voice to the experience of young Latina women. Like the author, her characters are bright, involved observers of their stimulating, colorful, and sometimes oppressive world. Among the honors her books have received are a **Before Columbus Foundation American Book Award** for *The House on Mango Street*, **PEN Center West Award** for Best Fiction for *Woman Hollering Creek*, and a Booklist **Editor's Choice** in the category Adult Fiction for Young Adults for *Caramelo*.

– R. C. Lutz

p.132

p.723

p.143

Beverly Cleary

Born: April 12, 1916; McMinnville, Oregon

www.beverlycleary.com

Known primarily as a writer of children's novels, **Beverly Cleary** is esteemed for her delightful portrayals of the small events in the daily lives of children. She does not back away from realistic situations but handles them with a light touch, believing that reading should be a joy and not a burden to children. Although she treats sensitive topics such as the pain of divorce and the uncertainty of unemployment, she also writes about newspaper routes, reading groups, and pets. In fact, she has written both the kinds of books that she most wanted to read when she was a child and the kinds of books that children asked for when she was a librarian. Along the way, she has created some of the most beloved characters in children's literature.

p.35

Cleary was born Beverly Bunn and began her life on a farm in the tiny town of Yamhill, not far from Portland, Oregon. Her mother started the local town's first library in a room above the bank. The family moved to Portland when Cleary reached school age. Despite her love of books, she found herself in her classes' lowest reading groups. However, by the time she reached third grade she was an accomplished reader and avid patron of the public library. She left Portland to attend college in California, where she met her husband, and she eventually received a **library degree** from the University of Washington. She has written of her early years in two wonderful memoirs: *A Girl from Yamhill* (1980) and *My Own Two Feet* (1995).

p.134

In 1950 Cleary wrote her first book, *Henry*

TITLES

Henry Huggins, 1950

Fifteen, 1956

Jean and Johnny, 1959

Ramona the Pest, 1968

Runaway Ralph, 1970

Ramona and Her Father, 1977

Ramona Quimby, Age Eight, 1981

Dear Mr. Henshaw, 1983

Ramona's World, 1999

School of Librarianship

The University of Washington School of Librarianship has existed since 1903 and the changes in the school over time reflect the changes in librarianship itself. As computers became crucial to library life, librarians began dealing with information in many different forms. In 1980, the name changed to the Graduate School of Library and Information Science. In 1997 the Master of Librarianship degree became the Master of Library and Information Science. In 2000, the school also offered a Bachelor of Science of Informatics, a PhD in Information Science, and a Master of Information Management. In 2001, the name of the school was changed to the Information School. Librarianship has become a highly specialized field.

Huggins, about an eight-year old boy living on Portland's Klickitat Street—a real street near where she grew up. Through the early 1960's, she continued writing about Henry; his dog, Ribsy; and his friend Beezus. In the late 1960's, she returned to the neighborhood to create the Ramona series. In fact, Cleary's most popular character is Ramona Quimby, the younger sister of Henry's pal Beezus. *Ramona the Pest*, the first of the series, follows Ramona through her kindergarten year, when she—as Cleary had done—struggles with reading, substitute teachers, and boys. Subsequent books deal with Ramona's father's unemployment, her aunt's marriage, and a new baby sister.

Cleary has also tried her hand at writing for an older market with books such as *Fifteen* and *Jean and Johnny*. She also ventured into **fantasy**, with *The Mouse and the Motorcycle* (1965), and *Runaway Ralph*, featuring the adventures of a motorcycle-riding mouse. In another departure from the Henry and Ramona books, she wrote *Dear Mr. Henshaw*, the story of a young boy growing up with the pain of divorce, told through his letters and diary entries.

p.87

National Medal of Arts

Established by Congress in 1984, the National Medal of Arts is awarded by the president of the United States to those who have made extraordinary contributions to the creation, growth, and support of the arts in the United States. Recipients of the medal are honored in a ceremony in the Oval Office of the White House.

Beverly Cleary is one of the most honored authors of books for young readers of her time. Both *Ramona and Her Father* and *Ramona Quimby, Age Eight* were

p.102

named as **Newbery Honor Books** and *Dear Mr. Henshaw* won the **Newbery Medal**. For her overall contributions to children's literature she has also re-

p.45

ceived the **American Library Association's Laura Ingalls Wilder Award**, the Catholic Li-brary Association's **Regina Medal**, and the Univer-

.252

sity of Southern Mississippi's **Silver Medallion**. She also was honored with the 2003 **National Medal of Arts**. The Beverly Cleary Sculpture Gar-

p.135

den, including bronze statues of Ramona, Henry, and Ribsy is located in Portland, Oregon, where both she and most of her characters grew up.

– Mary Virginia Davis

Lucille Clifton

Born: June 27, 1936; Depew, New York

www.math.buffalo.edu/~sww/clifton/clifton.html

A **Pulitzer Prize**-nominated poet and recipient of the 2000 **National Book Award** for Poetry for *Blessing the Boats*, African American writer **Lucille Clifton** has also achieved wide critical and popular acclaim for her juvenile books. She was also named the poet laureate for the state of Maryland in 1974.

Born Thelma Lucille Sayles in western New York, Clifton grew up in a large household of extended family members, including her grandparents and several uncles. The stories of her family's origins, particularly those of her great-grandmother, a former slave who escaped to the North, provided an early spark to Clifton's young imagination.

Clifton attended **Howard University** in p.138 Washington, D.C., with fellow students who included the future playwright and poet Amiri Baraka and the future **Nobel Prize-winning** novelist Toni p.231 Morrison. She developed an early interest in dramatic writing and acting. In 1958, she graduated and married Fred Clifton, with whom she had six children over the next seven years. In addition to raising her children and working full time, Clifton also began to write poetry. She published her first volume, *Good Times*, in 1969, followed by her poetry collections *Two-Headed Woman* (1980) and *Good Woman: Poems and a Memoir, 1969-1980* (1987). *Blessing the Boats* (2000), won the **National Book Award** for poetry.

In 1970 Clifton published *Some of the Days of Everett Anderson*, the first in a series of popular po-

▸ p.137
p.12

Pulitzer Prize

Joseph Pulitzer was an immigrant from Hungary who purchased the *St. Louis Post-Dispatch* and made it into a respected, investigative newspaper. Some years later, he purchased the *New York World*, where he worked the same magic. In his will, he established the Pulitzer Prize and the Columbia University School of Journalism to encourage excellence in journalism, American letters, and the arts. The Prize was first awarded in 1917 and now is awarded annually to 21 individuals: Journalists, photographers, novelists, historians, biographers, poets, and playwrights. Each winner receives a cash prize of $10,000 and is honored in a ceremony at Columbia University.

etry books that depicted Everett Anderson, a young African American boy, in different stages of his life. The book comprises nine poems that describe in verse a week in the life of its young **protagonist**, showing that some days are good, some bad, but all are important. Clifton's books in the Everett Anderson series celebrate the rich diversity of African American life and the importance of strong family ties. *Everett Anderson's Christmas Coming* features poems for each of the five days that Everett expectantly awaits for the arrival of Christmas. In *Everett Anderson's Goodbye*, which won the **American Library Association's Coretta Scott King Award**, Clifton uses her poetry to describe how Everett copes with the death of his father.

Clifton's books for children address specific issues within the

.233
p.45
p.66

Howard University

Howard University is the largest of the historically black colleges and universities in the U.S. It was founded in Washington, D.C., by a Congressional Act to provide education to freed slaves. It was originally intended as a seminary to train African American preachers, but then expanded to include the training of teachers. By the time it was chartered in 1867, it had become a full university. By 1900 the student body was 90 percent African American. Through the years Howard has gained a strong academic reputation and has educated some of the best known African American intellectuals and leaders in the country.

black community as well as broader themes common to children of all cultural backgrounds. *Sonora Beautiful* is a coming-of-age story about a teenage white girl who struggles with her sense of personal identity. In *My Friend Jacob* (1980), a young African American boy named Sam befriends a white teenage neighbor boy who suffers from a mental disability.

– Philip Bader

Barbara Cohen

Born: March 15, 1932; Ashbury Park, New Jersey
Died: November 29, 1992; Bridgewater, New Jersey

www.harperchildrens.com/teacher/catalog/
author_xml.asp?authorID=1865

Many of **Barbara Cohen**'s novels draw on her Jewish upbringing. Others draw on such diverse sources as the Bible, ancient Jewish history, and medieval works including Geoffrey Chaucer's late fourteenth century work, *The Canterbury Tales*. Her books humanize and fictionalize historical and biblical figures, bringing them into contexts to which modern readers can relate.

The daughter of innkeepers, Cohen married an innkeeper herself. After earning degrees from Barnard College and Rutgers University, she spent five years as a high school English teacher before realizing that she could support herself by writing.

One of Cohen's earliest books is an appreciation of Jackie Robinson's heroic entry into baseball as the first African American to play in the modern major leagues. *Thank You, Jackie Robinson*, an imaginary story about a young boy who takes a baseball to Robinson to have it signed, captures both the elation and the anguish Robinson felt as the first outsider in what had traditionally been a segregated sport. This story, reaching beyond the mere biographical, is important for its social and political contexts. Cohen authentically captures the temper of the period in which Robinson demolished old taboos and paved the way for minorities.

Cohen drew on Jewish history in *I Am Joseph*, a well-constructed version of ancient tales

p.396

of the Old Testament **Patriarchs** from an original and nontraditional point of view. As in most of her work, *I Am Joseph* depicts the biblical figures as characters with whom modern readers can relate. Among Cohen's books with a biographical emphasis *Yussel's Prayer: A Yom Kippur Story* is notable. *Here Come the Purim Players!* also represents a part of her canon that reflects her religious background.

Molly's Pilgrim is set during the 1940's. Molly, an immigrant child from Russia, is in the third grade and is about to spend her first Thanksgiving in the United States. Taunted by her classmates because of her accent, Molly is faced with the assignment of making a doll that will represent those who celebrated the first Thanksgiving in North America. Not knowing what she is to do, her lack of understanding separates her still more completely from her classmates. Cohen presents Molly's mother as a sensitive and supportive parent and depicts Molly's bewilderment and isolation compassionately. This novel, made into a short film written and directed by Jeff Brown, was nominated for an Academy Award for the best live action short subject of 1985.

In *Make a Wish, Molly* the sequel to *Molly's Pilgrim*, Emma, Molly's best friend, invites Molly to her birthday party. Eager to attend, Molly longs to sample the pink birthday cake that Emma promises. Molly's mother reminds her, however, that the party falls during **Passover**, when Jews must eat only

p.141

The Canterbury Tales

Geoffrey Chaucer wrote *The Canterbury Tales* between 1380 and 1400. It is one of the classics of English literature. It is a collection of stories told by a group of travelers on a pilgrimage to the shrine of St. Thomas in Canterbury, England. As they stop for the night, their host proposes a storytelling competition. Their stories and interaction with one another continue to delight readers more than six hundred years after they were created.

Passover

Passover is a Jewish holiday celebrated in March or April. It celebrates God's delivering of the Jewish people from slavery in Egypt more than three thousand years ago, as told in the biblical book of Exodus. A special service and meal, called a Seder, begins the eight days of Passover. During this time, Jewish people do not eat any leavened food—food in which yeast or baking soda lightens the dough or batter. Matzo, an unleavened bread made simply from flour and water, is served; this is the bread that the Jews made for their hurried flight from Egypt.

Passover food. Molly, though distressed that her mother does not understand American ways, in the end cannot bring herself to violate her religious traditions. Several days later Emma comes by with two friends, and they celebrate Molly's birthday with her by eating freshly baked rugelach pastries. Molly awakens to the realization that one can have different traditions and still fit in with others. She also gains a renewed appreciation of her mother.

– R. Baird Shuman

Brock Cole

Born: May 29, 1938; Charlotte, Michigan

www.edupaperback.org/showauth2.cfm?authid=123

Brock Cole confronts adult themes in his young adult fiction. His no-holds-barred prose has both won critical acclaim and engendered controversy. Cole has said that the challenges of fiction are the same no matter what the age of the readers. His young characters must survive—both physically and emotionally—complex, sometimes brutal, encounters with sexual abuse, domestic violence, neglect, betrayal, and even murder.

The Goats established Cole as a preeminent writer of young adult fiction. Its main characters, Howie and Laura, are social outcasts who are humiliated by a cruel prank. At summer camp, their peers take them to Goat Island and abandon them. Instead of crawling back to camp in shame, they decide to escape from the island on their own and live by their wits. The relationship that develops between Howie and Laura is rich with subtleties of blossoming adolescent sexuality. Their travels take them across a considerable geographical distance; more importantly, they travel within themselves to discover strengths they never knew they had.

The hero of *Celine* is a sixteen-year-old high school girl. A talented artist and gifted student, Celine lives with her professor father who, after divorcing her mother, marries one of his students who is only six years older than Celine. Celine wants only

Booklist

This magazine published by the American Library Association reviews more than 4,000 adult books, 2,500 children's books, 500 reference books, and 1,000 audiovisual materials for librarians each year. In addition, it offers special features such as lists of the best books on a particular subject. It also publishes an annual Editor's Choice list of the best books in a given year. The *Booklist* reviews are respected by librarians for their insight and evaluation.

to graduate from high school early and escape to live in Europe. In her first-person narrative, she quips and jokes her way past obstacle after obstacle. She is a study in contrasts: mature and self-reliant one minute, childish and wayward the next. Like *The Goats*, this is a coming-of-age novel, and Celine derives much of her burgeoning maturity from a friendship with eight-year-old Jake, a lonely child of separated parents who lives in a neighboring apartment.

The Facts Speak for Themselves has been both praised and criticized for its raw subject matter and stark, reportorial voice. In a first-person narrative, thirteen-year-old Linda reveals how she has gotten involved in the murder of one man and the suicide of another. It soon becomes apparent that adult behaviors and responsibilities have been forced upon her, both by her drunken and irresponsible mother and by an older man who sexually abuses her. Cole is both a writer and **illustrator**. The jacket illustration for this book is Cole's own stark portrait of a young woman emerging scarred, but strong, from the wreckage of her childhood.

Brock Cole's larger-than-life plots, fully drawn

p.38

characters, deft humor, and controversial themes have earned the author numerous awards. *The Goats* was a *School Library Journal* **Best Book of the Year** and a *Booklist* **Best Book** of the 1980's. *Celine* was named a **Best Book for Young Adults** by the American Library Association. *The Facts Speak for Themselves* was a finalist for a **National Book Award** and a *Publishers Weekly* **Best Book** of 1997.

– Faith Hickman Brynie

p.195
p.143
p.480
p.122
p.4
p.144

James Lincoln Collier

Born: June 27, 1928; New York, New York

www.randomhouse.com/kids/author/
results_spotlight.perl?authorid=5394

James Lincoln Collier worked as a magazine **editor** before publishing his first book in 1965. A lifelong musician, he writes nonfiction books about music, especially **jazz**; however, the books that young readers most love are the historical novels that he often writes with his brother, Christopher Collier.

Collier had two children before he was divorced and thus knows how teenagers can suffer. He often focuses on his characters' conflicts with their parents. His young adult books are suspenseful, fast-paced, humorous, and compassionate. *The Teddy Bear Habit* is a favorite for many teenagers. A twelve-year-old boy has a lot of problems, such as his "square" music lessons, his attachment to his childhood teddy bear, and his father who earns a living creating comic strips. To break his dull routine, he gets involved with jewel thieves, with surprising results. In *Rich and Famous*, George suddenly finds himself the darling of a New York television company that plans to transform him into a singing, guitar-playing teenage idol. Many crazy adventures await him.

The Colliers have written dozens of books about history, and their characters are likeable and believable. *My Brother Sam Is Dead* is a realistic story about the American Revolutionary War. Tragedy strikes the Meeker family when one son joins the rebel forces, while the rest of the family tries to remain neutral in a Tory-controlled town. In *The Winter Hero*, Justin explains how he becomes involved in

p.20
p.405
p.117

TITLES

The Teddy Bear Habit; Or, How I Became a Winner, 1967

Rock Star, 1970

Why Does Everybody Think I'm Nutty?, 1971

It's Murder at St. Basket's, 1972

My Brother Sam Is Dead, 1974 (with Christopher Collier)

Rich and Famous: The Further Adventures of George Stable, 1975

The Bloody Country, 1976 (with Christopher Collier)

Give Dad My Best, 1976

The Winter Hero, 1978 (with Christopher Collier)

Jump Ship to Freedom, 1981 (with Christopher Collier)

Planet Out of the Past, 1983

War Comes to Willy Freeman, 1983 (with Christopher Collier)

Who Is Carrie?, 1984 (with Christopher Collier)

When the Stars Begin to Fall, 1986

Outside Looking In, 1987

The Winchesters, 1988

My Crooked Family, 1991

p.146

Shays's Rebellion, in which Massachusetts farmers fight against taxes imposed on them by the Boston government. In *Jump Ship to Freedom*, fourteen-year-old slave Daniel Arabus will do anything to buy freedom for himself and his mother, including escaping from his dishonest master and fighting in the war. In *War Comes to Willy Freeman*, a thirteen-year-old girl is terrified of being returned to slavery when her patriot father is killed by the British.

Collier's themes include social hypocrisy and environmentalism. In *When the Stars Begin to Fall*, fourteen-year-old Harry is angry and frustrated that his family is considered poor trash, so he defies his father and sets out to prove that a factory is polluting their **Adirondack** village. In *Outside Looking In*, Fergy takes his young sister and runs away to find a better life because he is ashamed that his parents travel around like thievish gypsies. Similarly, *The Winchesters* tells about fourteen-year-old Chris, a poor relation of the wealthy Winchesters, who must chose to side with either management or labor when his classmates' parents go on strike at the Winchester mill to get better wages. In *My Crooked Family*, thirteen-year-old Roger lives with irresponsible parents on the seedy side of town in 1910, falls in with a gang of murderous burglars, and discovers a

The Adirondacks

The Adirondacks refers to a region in Northern New York state the includes the Adirondack Mountains and Adirondack Park. It is an area rich with lakes, hiking trails, resorts, and campgrounds. The six million acre park was created in 1882 by the New York state legislature to guarantee that wild lands would be protected. Unlike many parks, this one also includes private lands. It is possible to hike in the wilderness by day and enjoy dinner in a small village by night.

Phoenix Award

The Phoenix Award was created in 1985 by the Children's Literature Association, an organization of teachers, scholars, librarians, editors, writers, illustrators, and parents interested in promoting the study of literature. It is awarded each year to the author of a book previously published in English but not given the critical attention it deserves. Hence, the name "Phoenix," the legendary bird that rises from the ashes to live again.

shocking secret about his father. Things are hard for fifteen-year-old Annie in 1810 in *The Clock*, when she is trapped in a horrible job at a Connecticut textile mill, becomes the victim of the cruel overseer, and plots revenge against him.

James Collier knows how to write exciting books that readers have trouble putting down. His writing honors include a **Newbery Honor Book** award for *My Brother Sam Is Dead*, which also received a **Phoenix Award** and was nominated for a **National Book Award**.

p.102

p.122

p.147

– Fiona Kelleghan

Carolyn Coman

Born: August 12, 1929; Evanston, Illinois

www.teenreads.com/authors/au-coman-carolyn.asp

Carolyn Coman's novels focus on families caught up in hopeless cycles of miscommunication, mistrust, and unacknowledged fears. Acts of violence—murder, tragic accidents, even incest—set her plots into motion. Her young characters are typically betrayed by the adults in their lives, adults who are not wholly cruel, but who have made selfish or misguided choices that endanger their children physically or emotionally. The confused and often angry young characters, whose inner landscapes Coman reveals clearly, make clumsy attempts to cope as they move from darkness into light, from instability to stability, from anger to forgiveness.

After graduating from Hampshire College in Massachusetts, Coman worked as a hand **book-binder** and later as an editor of children's educational materials. She dreamed of becoming a writer from the time she was in the fourth grade. Ultimately, the desire to write became stronger than her fear of failure. p.149

Coman is interested in showing how her characters work out difficulties, and her novels reveal a profound respect for the emotional integrity of young people. In *Tell Me Everything*, twelve-year-old Roz is obsessed with finding the boy her mother was trying to rescue in an avalanche when she died. p.90 She runs away from her uncle-guardian, an emotionally isolated **Vietnam War** veteran, to seek answers. In the end, she finds her answers not with the boy but with her uncle Mike, who helps her to accept her mother's death and to face life.

Bee and Jacky also depicts confused children living with a taciturn Vietnam veteran. After the children's father is wounded in Vietnam, the children are set on a path of mutual self-destruction when their childhood games in the woods—reenactments of the battles in Vietnam—turn incestuous. When the parents leave for a weekend, the brother and sister, now teenagers, confront the truth of their relationship. After putting an end to her inappropriate intimacy with her brother, Bee discovers a mystical light emanating from her dark, confused being. The novel, on one level painfully realistic, is overlaid with a strong current of **Magical Realism**.

 p.362

Many Stones focuses on high school swimmer Berry Morgan, who has survived her father's desertion and the murder of her older sister, Laura, in South Africa. The novel opens after these events have occurred. Angry at her father and unable to accept Laura's death, Berry becomes increasingly uninterested in her own life; she gives in to an intimate relationship with a boy whom she does not love and quits her swimming team. A return trip to 150 **South Africa** with her father to present a gift to the school where Laura worked precipitates a painful reconciliation with her womanizing, selfish, but ultimately deeply caring father and, in the process, an acceptance of Laura's death.

Carolyn Coman also teaches children's writing at Vermont College and writes books

Bookbinding

When a book is printed, the last step is to attach the covers to the block of pages. The pages are either sewn or glued into a block. With a paperback book, the covers can be automatically applied by machinery. With a hardcover book, it is often necessary to use a binding machine to apply the covers and spine. Traditionally, covers of books were applied by hand work, and in some fine art presses, hand bookbinding is still done today.

Apartheid

The history of South Africa is defined by apartheid (the Afrikaans word meaning "apart-ness") which was the policy of segregation in the Republic of South Africa that was aimed at non-white native groups. It involved racial, political, and economic discrimination. This segregation of black Africans and white Africans was present from the time of the

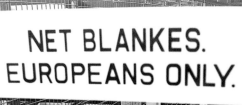

first European settlers. It became stricter in 1948 when an Afrikaans government was elected. These white South Africans of Dutch heritage prohibited mixed marriages and assigned every South African to a defined racial group. Black Africans continued to be banned from the government and from owning land. Beginning in 1989, with the election of white South African F.W. de Klerk as president, this policy began to change. He called for an end to discrimination. In 1994, the first non-racial elections were held and Nelson Mandela, a black African activist, was elected to the national presidency.

for children. Her *What Jamie Saw* (1995) is an emotionally evocative novel that broke new ground in discussing child abuse at a level appropriate for young children. It was named a **Newbery Honor Book** and a **National Book Award** finalist. Coman's *Many Stones* was honored by the **American Library Association's Best Books for Young Adults** award; it was also a **Michael L. Printz Honor Book** and a **National Book Award** finalist.

p.102

p.45

p.488

p.12

p.480

p.12

– Jan Allister

Ellen Conford

Born: March 20, 1942; New York, New York

Ellen Conford's ability to blend humor with the emotional difficulties of teenage life has characterized her long career of writing for young people. Her main characters, most often teenage girls, are typically forced to discover the difference between fantasy and reality, especially in matters of love. Along the way, they encounter hilarious situations and learn that it is important to look beneath the surface when forming relationships.

Born Ellen Schaffer, Conford began writing poetry in elementary school and was encouraged by teachers and family to develop her writing abilities. She later enrolled at Hofstra College and soon married a fellow student. She left school a few years later to have a baby. While searching for good books to read to her young son, she concluded that she could write better books than those that were being published for children. Her first picture books appeared shortly thereafter.

Conford eventually began writing for an older audience. In her novel *Dear Lovey Hart, I Am Desperate*, a girl named Carrie becomes the anonymous advice columnist for her high school paper and manages to solve everyone's problems but her own. In the sequel, *We Interrupt This Semester for an Important Bulletin*, Carrie becomes an **investigative reporter** for the school paper while competing for the attentions of Chip, the paper's editor. *The Alfred G. Graebner Memorial High School Handbook of Rules and Regulations* utilizes a different format, with a chapter devoted to each school rule, all of which are

.152

ridiculously out of touch with the reality of high school as experienced by sophomore Julie.

Some of Conford's young adult novels feature protagonists in less realistic but equally humorous situations. In *You Never Can Tell*, Kate has the opportunity to compare a soap opera hunk with his real-life alter ego when the young actor leaves his show and enrolls in her high school. In *A Royal Pain*, Kansas teenager Abby is astonished to learn that she is a princess in line for the throne of a small European country. *Genie with the Light Blue Hair* has a girl named Jean receive a magic lamp as a birthday present. She soon discovers that having a personal genie is not as easy as it sounds.

p.233

Conford's other books feature characters attempting to improve themselves or attract members of the opposite sex. In *Seven Days to a Brand-New Me*, Maddy tries to recreate herself with the aid of a self-help book. In *The Things I Did for Love*, Stephanie begins investigating love and romance for a psychology assignment and conducts some personal research. *Why Me?* features a male protagonist, Hobie, who is caught up in a string of unrequited crushes, while Joey in *Strictly for Laughs* is a budding comedienne who finds it diffi-

Parents' Choice Award

The Parents' Choice Foundation was founded in 1978 as a not-for-profit evaluator of children's books, videos, audios, toys, computer software, television programs, and magazines. The Parents' Choice Award is given to less than 15% of the products submitted for the foundation's evaluation. Products can receive the award in one of six levels: Classic, Gold, Silver, Recommended, Approved, and Fun Stuff. The award indicates a product that helps children's intellectual, emotional, and social growth.

cult to show her serious feelings for Peter. In addition to novels, Conford published *Crush*, a set of linked short stories about a group of friends trying to line up dates for a Valentine's Day dance.

Ellen Conford's ability to write engaging romantic comedies about teens has earned her several awards, including the Parents' Choice Award for both *Why Me?* and *A Royal Pain*.

p.153

– Amy Sisson

Caroline B. Cooney

Born: May 10, 1947; Greenwich, Connecticut

www.teenreads.com/authors/au-cooney-
caroline.asp#pastview

Caroline B. Cooney specializes in novels for young adults that combine suspense with contemporary teenage issues. Having raised three teenagers of her own, she has an excellent insight into their problems and concerns. Although she realizes that styles change with time, the core issues important to young people never go out of date.

Cooney was born and reared in Greenwich, Connecticut, and was an avid reader who loved school. Deeply involved in music, she played piano and organ for church and school productions, and even directed a choir. After graduating from high school in 1965, she attended several colleges, studying music, art, English, and nursing. Although she never graduated, she discovered a talent for writing during her college years. In 1967 she married and had the first of her three children at the age of twenty-one. While at home with the children she began writing short stories and eventually had one accepted by *Seventeen* magazine. She went on to publish her first book in 1979.

Among Cooney's most popular books are those in her Janie series. The first of the series, *The Face on the Milk Carton*, tells the story of fifteen-year-old Janie Johnson, who recognizes herself in the photo of a missing child on a milk carton, causing her to question her true identity and investigate her past. *Whatever Happened to Janie?* explores what happens when Janie goes to live with her biological p.155 family. *The Voice on the Radio* finds Janie betrayed by her boyfriend who reveals her story on his college radio show to attract more listeners. Finally, *What Janie Found* brings the story full circle as Janie goes in search of Hannah, her kidnapper.

Driver's Ed explores the consequences for Remy and her high school crush Morgan when their prank of stealing a stop sign results in the death of a young mother at the same intersection later the same night. The theme of an innocent prank backfiring resonates strongly with young adult readers. *Twenty Pageants Later* explores the world of teen beauty pageants as eighth grader Scottie-Ann, whose beautiful older sister is a pageant veteran, is forced to compete in her own school-sponsored pageant. Although Cooney portrays the backbiting jealousy of pageant contestants and the pushy behavior of parents, she also reveals that pageants have their benefits as well. *Don't Blame the Music* deals with a family torn apart by their burned-out twenty-five-year-old rock-star daughter's return home. The family must confront the fact that their daughter's violent behavior, particularly against her younger sister Susan, indicates a serious mental problem.

DNA Fingerprinting

DNA fingerprinting includes a variety of techniques in which individuals are identified using DNA sequences. In humans, more than 99% of all DNA is identical, so scientists focus on the small regions of DNA that are known to vary from individual to individual. By using a variety of tests, scientists are able to determine whether a child's parents are the biological parents or whether the child is genetically related to another couple.

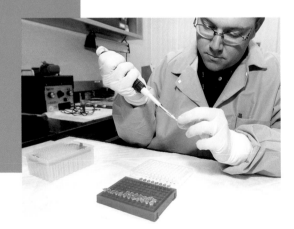

The New York Public Library

Founded in 1895, The New York Public Library is a remarkable institution. It is located on Fifth Avenue in the heart of Manhattan, with majestic lions flanking the entrance. More than 15 million people use the services of the library at this and other locations each year. The library was founded when Samuel Tilden, a former governor of New York, left

the bulk of his fortune to establish a free library and reading room. His gift was merged with two private libraries to form a foundation. Today, the library is a privately managed nonprofit corporation using private and public funds to provide free access to the collection of the four research libraries and the eighty-five branch libraries.

p.45
p.156
p.480
p.14
p.45

Cooney received an American Library Association **Best Book for Young Adults** and a Booklist **Children's Editor's Choice** award for *Driver's Ed*, and a New York Public Library **Best Book for the Teen Age** for *Among Friends*. She also received an American Library Association **Quick Pick for Young Adults** for *Twenty Pageants Later*.

– Mary Virginia Davis

Susan Cooper

Born: May 23, 1935; Burnham, Buckinghamshire, England

www.thelostland.com/welcome.htm

p.87

p104.

.173

p.18

p.48

Susan Cooper's fantasy novels have been compared to those of **J. R. R. Tolkien** and C. S. Lewis, under whom she studied while she was a student at **Oxford University** in the 1950's. Half of Cooper's family background is Welsh. Two grandparents, an aunt, and at one time her parents lived in Aberdyfi, a town in central **Wales** on Cardigan Bay. As a consequence, Welsh **Arthurian** mythology deeply informs her novels.

Cooper started writing as a child and continued throughout college, where she became the first female editor of her school newspaper. After she graduated, she worked as a newspaper columnist and for **Ian Fleming**, the famous author who created the fictional superspy James Bond. After publishing an adult fantasy novel, she was inspired by a publisher's contest to try her hand at children's fiction. Although her entry did not win (and was even rejected by twenty publishers), the story finally was published as *Over Sea, Under Stone*. This book proved to be the first novel in her Dark Is Rising sequence.

p.158

In the meantime, Cooper married Nicholas Grant, an American scientist who taught at the Massachusetts Institute of Technology, near Boston, where she settled with him. She continued writing as a correspondent and columnist for British newspapers, but the mythological world she had evoked in *Over Sea, Under Stone* drew her back into fiction,

TITLES

The Dark Is Rising series:

Over Sea, Under Stone, 1965

The Dark Is Rising, 1973

Greenwitch, 1974

The Grey King, 1975

Silver on the Tree, 1977

Seaward, 1983

King of Shadows, 1999

and she eventually wrote sequels to that novel in what she called the Dark Is Rising series. After twenty years of marriage, she and Grant divorced. She then got involved in theater and began collaborating with actor **Hume Cronyn**, whom she married in 1996. p.159

Cooper's The Dark Is Rising sequence is based on characters and events in Welsh mythology that are the source material from which later medieval romances about England's legendary King Arthur were drawn. However, her main characters and much of the action in the books are set in the twentieth century. *Over Sea, Under Stone* is the story of the three Drew children, Simon, Jane, and Barney, who discover a map that leads them to the **Holy Grail** in p.717 the attic of their great-uncle Merriman Lyon—who turns out to be Merlin. The children fall prey to forces of the Dark before the Grail is recovered and placed in the British Museum, and the manuscript that holds the key to its mysteries is sent to the bottom of the sea.

The next book in the series, *The Dark Is Rising*, involves Will Stanton, who discovers that he is the

Ian Fleming

Ian Fleming was born in 1908 to a wealthy, socially prominent British family. His father died when he was young, and he spent his youth trying to live up to his father's and older brother's reputations. Ian developed a love of high living, traveling, romancing, and partying. After a brief career in banking, Fleming returned to an on-again off-again career as a journalist. He also worked as a spy for the Naval Intelligence service during World War II. Near the end of the war, Fleming traveled to the tropical island paradise of Jamaica, and after the war he built his home, Goldeneye, there. It was there that he wrote his first James Bond thriller in 1952. For the next twelve years, he would continue to write about his famous character and spend winters in Jamaica. His high living came at a price. In 1964 at the age of 56 he died from a bad heart. His life seems to have been the inspiration for the character of James Bond.

Hume Cronyn

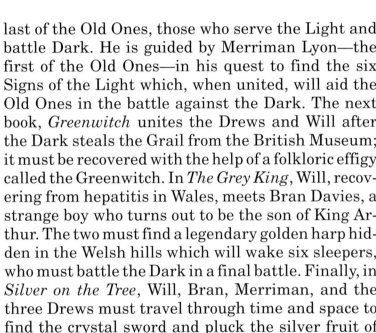

Hume Cronyn was born in Canada in 1911. He began acting when he was nineteen years old and went on to become one of the best known actors on the stage and screen. In 1942 he married the actress Jessica Tandy, and they were to act on stage and in movies until her death in 1994. That same year they were given a Tony Award for lifetime theatrical achievement. In 1996, Cronyn married author and playwright Susan Cooper. She was a long-time family friend who had collaborated with Cronyn and Tandy on several theater works. Cronyn died in 2003.

last of the Old Ones, those who serve the Light and battle Dark. He is guided by Merriman Lyon—the first of the Old Ones—in his quest to find the six Signs of the Light which, when united, will aid the Old Ones in the battle against the Dark. The next book, *Greenwitch* unites the Drews and Will after the Dark steals the Grail from the British Museum; it must be recovered with the help of a folkloric effigy called the Greenwitch. In *The Grey King*, Will, recovering from hepatitis in Wales, meets Bran Davies, a strange boy who turns out to be the son of King Arthur. The two must find a legendary golden harp hidden in the Welsh hills which will wake six sleepers, who must battle the Dark in a final battle. Finally, in *Silver on the Tree*, Will, Bran, Merriman, and the three Drews must travel through time and space to find the crystal sword and pluck the silver fruit of the Midsummer Tree in order to prevent the Dark from finally overwhelming the world.

Susan Cooper's writing honors include a **Boston Globe-Horn Book** and **Newbery Honor Book** awards for *The Dark Is Rising*, a **Newbery Medal** for *The Grey King*, and an **American Library Association Best Books for Young Adults** award for *King of Shadows*.

— Leslie Ellen Jones

.747   p.102   p.45   p.480

Robert Cormier

Born: January 17, 1925; Leominster, Massachusetts
Died: November 2, 2000; Boston, Massachusetts
www.teenreads.com/authors/au-cormier-robert.asp

Robert Cormier's writing is distinguished for its realistic portrayal of adolescents facing moral challenges in a threatening world. His young protagonists are frequently the victims of hypocritical or ineffectual adults as well as manipulative peers. They usually find themselves alone in their struggles to uphold their principles in unsupportive environments, and this leads them to question society's values.

p.233

Robert Edmund Cormier was born near Boston, Massachusetts. From an early age he preferred reading to the activities that engaged most of the children in his working-class neighborhood. By the time he entered college, he knew that he wanted to be a writer. He made his first professional fiction sale at the age of eighteen.

Cormier was a father of four and a professional journalist with three published novels to his credit when, in 1974, he wrote *The Chocolate War*, his first novel for young readers. His inspiration was the experience of his son, who refused on principle to sell chocolates at a fund-raising event for his high school. In the novel, Cormier portrays the sale of chocolates to benefit a Roman Catholic school as an event crucial to the private agendas of the school's headmaster and the leader of a secret student society, both of whom are ambitious and unscrupulous. When Jerry Renault, a first-year student, declines to sell the chocolates, they resort to peer pressure and physical intimidation to break his spirit and teach other students a lesson about the price of individuality.

After *The Chocolate War* was a big success, Cormier focused his interests as a writer on the problems of adolescents in a world depicted as challenging and full of moral uncertainties. His next novel, *I Am the Cheese*, is a tale of psychological suspense, told from the point of view of a teenage boy whose life and sanity are imperiled when his journalist father exposes political corruption, forcing the family to hide their identities through the help of a witness protection program. *After the First Death* is another novel in which Cormier explores the high cost of personal ideals and the difficult moral choices that children and adults must make. It is about an effort to rescue a school bus full of children taken captive by terrorists.

p.161

In a career as a writer for young adults that spanned more than a quarter century, Cormier explored the emotional and psychological geography of his teenage characters through largely realistic plots concerned with juvenile delinquency (*We All Fall Down*), racial prejudice (*Tunes for Bears to Dance To*), and hero worship and disillusionment (*Heroes*). *Fade*, which is about a boy who must decide whether to use his talent for becoming invisible for good or bad purposes, is his sole excursion into fantasy.

p.87

Robert Cormier's fiction has met with controversy because of its frankness, its negative depic-

Witness Protection Programs

Witness protection programs provide security for witnesses whose testimony is necessary in high risk or dangerous court cases. While some states have state-managed programs, the most frequently used program is the Federal Witness Protection Program, which began in 1970. Designed to combat organized crime, this program has provided security and even fake identities for more than 5,000 witnesses. Beyond providing for the physical safety of witnesses, the program also provides health care, relocation services, psychological support, and social adjustment aid.

Assembly on Literature for Adolescents

ALAN was founded in 1973 as a part of the National Council of Teachers of English (NCTE), a professional organization. Members of ALAN are teachers, authors, librarians, and publishers. Each November at the ALAN breakfast at the NCTE national convention, members present an award to the publisher, author, librarian, scholar, editor, or active member of the organization who has made an outstanding contribution to adolescent literature for that year.

tions of authority figures, and its unflinching portrayals of cruelty, isolation, and disenchantment as common to adolescent experiences. Nevertheless, his books were frequently selected as *New York Times* notables, and he was awarded the **Assembly on Literature for Adolescents Award** by the National Council of Teachers of English for his distinguished contributions to young adult literature. His many other writing honors include the 1991 **Margaret A. Edwards Award** for Outstanding Literature for Young Adults. His books have been translated into many languages, and several have been adapted for film.

— Stefan Dziemianowicz

Stephen Crane

Born: November 1, 1871; Newark, New Jersey
Died: June 5, 1900; Badenweiler, Germany

guweb2.gonzaga.edu/faculty/campbell/crane/
index.html

Although **Stephen Crane** earned critical acclaim from such literary figures as Hamlin Garland and W. D. Howells for the social realism of his first novel, *Maggie: A Girl of the Streets*, it was not until his publication of *The Red Badge of Courage* in 1895 that he was recognized as an important American author. At the age of twenty-four, Crane found himself famous for writing this extraordinary coming-of-age novel set during the American Civil War. Its **protagonist**, Henry Fleming, fantasizes about fighting bravely in battle as the Greek heroes had done in the ancient past. He enlists in the Union Army in order to raise himself above mediocrity and cleanse himself of all self-doubt.

Born in Newark, New Jersey, Crane was the fourteenth child of Reverend Jonathan Crane and Mary Peck Crane. It was difficult for Crane's father to support such a large family. Although he grew up in a Christian home, Crane would struggle with spiritual matters through most of his short life. By 1891 he was writing sketches about urban life. He came to believe that poverty would help nurture his creativity. Although he was able to sell some of his sketches to the *New York Herald*, he remained poor. He eventually

.233▶

.164▶

TITLES

Maggie: A Girl of the Streets, 1893

The Red Badge of Courage: An Episode of the American Civil War, 1895

The New York Herald

The New York Herald was one of the great newspapers in U.S. history. It was founded in 1835 by James Gordon Bennett. Under his son, in 1869, the paper financed the excursion of U.S. newsman Henry Morton Stanley into Africa to find the famed British explorer David Livingstone. "Dr. Livingstone, I presume?" were the famous first words uttered by the journalist upon finding the long-lost explorer. In 1887, Bennett, Jr., launched a European edition in Paris. Following his death in 1922, the paper was merged with *The New York Tribune* and became *The New York Herald Tribune*. In 1966, the New York newpaper stopped publication and *The New York Times* and *The Washington Post* took control of the Paris edition, renaming it the *International Herald Tribune*, which is now owned exclusively by The New York Times company.

would die at the age of twenty-eight in Badenweiler, Germany, exhausted from leading a turbulent and intense life.

Crane's first novel, *Maggie*, is an unflinching look at slum life. The title character is a young Irish American girl who attempts to make her way in New York City. Circumstances conspire against her and she becomes a prostitute. Ultimately, she chooses to throw herself into the East River and end her short sad life. Crane paints a bleak picture of life in the slums and does not give Maggie an escape route out of her desperate situation other than suicide.

The Red Badge of Courage, Crane's masterpiece, was an international **best-seller**. It was praised for looking at war from the perspective of a foot soldier, rather than that of commanding officers. The novel does not concern itself with military tactics or troop movements. Crane places the reader in the battle by tracing the emotional impact of combat on a raw young recruit. The prose style of the

p.384

novel has been called impressionistic realism, and the novel is composed of various snapshots of war.

Although not specifically mentioned, it has been surmised that the battle central to *The Red Badge of Courage* is the Battle of Chancellorsville. Crane p.165 was not specific on this count in the novel in order to focus on psychological elements and not history. Young readers have been drawn to the novel because they can identify with the young inexperienced Union Army recruit, Henry Fleming, who must wrestle with fear, cowardice, arrogance, and the illusions of youth. Fleming can be viewed as an "everyman" who was once untested but now wears the "red badge of courage."

– Jeffry Jensen

Battle of Chancellorsville

During the Civil War, in 1863, the Union's Major General Joseph Hooker formulated an excellent tactical plan. He would hold the Confederate General Robert E. Lee's army near Fredericksburg, Virginia, with 40,000 troops under John Sedgwick while he marched around Lee's left flank with 75,000 troops. If Lee moved against Hooker, Sedgwick would advance against the Confederate rear. Intially, the plan worked perfectly, but on May 1, Confederates struck the advancing Union soldiers near Chancellorsville, named for a large brick tavern that marked an important road junction in the surrounding wilderness. Hooker retreated into the woods. On May 2, "Stonewall" Jackson and 28,000 Confederates marched across and around the Union front and delivered an early evening surprise attack. Lee renewed his attack on May 3, causing Hooker to retreat. Then he marched back toward Fredericksburg and stopped Sedgwick. This defeat of an army twice its size was Lee's greatest battle. Jackson died on May 10 of wounds suffered in the battle.

Sharon Creech

Born: July 29, 1945; South Euclid, Ohio

www.sharoncreech.com

Most of **Sharon Creech**'s young adult novels have as their central characters girls around the age of thirteen who go on journeys that lead them to discoveries about themselves and their families. Their journeys may be either literal or figurative and are often both. Creech's characters have realistic emotions and likeable personalities, and her stories have intriguing plots lines. All these characteristics make her novels compelling. She wrote two novels for adults before writing for young people. She has also written for younger children; *Love that Dog* (2001) has received especially wide critical acclaim.

Creech was born near Cleveland, Ohio, and grew up in a family of five children. She became interested in writing while attending college. Later, she taught high school English and writing at schools in England and Switzerland. During this time, she began writing fiction.

Creech has said that her book *Absolutely Normal Chaos* is a fictionalized account of her childhood family. The brothers in that book even have the names of her own brothers. The central character in the novel, Mary Lou records in her journal the emotional turmoil of adolescence over the course of a summer. Her concerns make interesting reading because they are so typical, such as her first kiss and her strained relationships with other family members. Mary Lou analyzes events in her life by thinking about the ancient Greek poet Homer's *Odyssey* p.167 and other literary works on her summer reading list.

Creech's own family took car trips during most

The Odyssey

Homer, an ancient Greek poet, is thought to have composed this epic some 2,800 years ago. It was originally sung or recited and was based on legend, folk tale, and invention. It is the story of Odysseus's journey home after the end of the famous Greek Trojan War. Odysseus was the ruler of the island kingdom of Ithaca and one of the most important leaders in the war. He was also the creator of the huge Trojan horse, with which the city of Troy was finally won. While the action of the homecoming occupies only a few weeks, Odysseus tells in fantastic detail what happened during his ten years away. It is the most popular epic in Western literature and has inspired writers throughout history.

of the summers when she was a child, and the places she visited figure prominently in her novels. The family often visited relatives in Quincy, Kentucky, which she transformed into Bybanks, Kentucky, in *Walk Two Moons*, *Chasing Redbird*, *Bloomability*, and *The Wanderer*. In *Chasing Redbird*, Zinnia explores an old trail near her home in Bybanks. The journey connects her to her ancestors who used the trail; she also makes it her own not only by clearing it again but also by planting zinnias along the way. *Bloomability* draws on Creech's experience of living abroad. In this novel, Dinnie attends **boarding school** in Switzerland. There, she grows up in ways that will help her p.168 cope with family complications at home.

Walk Two Moons, which was awarded the **Newbery Medal** and was chosen an **American Library Association** **Notable Children's Book**, p.102 p.45

tells of Sal's search for her mother. During the journey from Ohio to Idaho, Sal tells the story of another girl's search for her mother. The novel's interwoven plots and emotional complexity create an intricate and powerful story. The end of the novel reveals that Sal's mother has died. Coping with the loss of parents and connecting to other family members is also a theme in *The Wanderer* and *Ruby Holler*. In *The Wanderer*, Sophie records her thoughts on her parents' deaths in journal entries she writes while on a transatlantic sailboat journey. In *Ruby Holler*, an elderly couple adopts twins, and the four people slowly grow into a real family.

– Joan Hope

Helen Cresswell

Born: July 11, 1934; Nottinghamshire, England

Helen Cresswell's success as a writer has been helped by her involvement with British television. She began with a commission to write for *Jackanory*, a show in which stories were read aloud to young viewers. The Lizzie Dripping comedies that she wrote for that show were similar to her earlier comedies featuring Jumbo Spencer. She has also written many other comedies for young readers, as well as poetic fantasies. Her most widely read young adult books are those which have been dramatized for television, including *Moondial* and early episodes from the Bagthorpe Saga.

In 1967 Cresswell published her first book for young adults, *The Piemakers*. A family of caterers is disgraced by the failure of its first job to bake for royalty. They determine to make amends by producing the largest pie in history. This book established a pattern for a series of novels in which eccentric **artisans** obsessively apply themselves to odd projects showing the world of work as seen from an adolescent point of view. *The Signposters* expands the formula, while *The Night-Watchmen* cheerfully subverts it. *The Beachcombers* extends the formula in a surreal allegory whose young hero must decide whether to throw in his lot with the romantic seafaring Dallakers or the realistic landbound Pickerings. *The Bongleweed* is a marvelous invader, woefully underappreciated by adult gardeners and scientists despite the encouragement it receives from the young heroine of the novel.

Cresswell's Bagthorpe Saga, which she began

with *Ordinary Jack* and *Absolute Zero*, is a flamboyant family farce whose episodes each cover a few days in an unfolding narrative. Mr. Bagthorpe is a hot tempered television scriptwriter cursed with an extended family, which "attracts calamity as a flagpole attracts lightning." His wife is an advice columnist and justice of the peace. His parents are completely irresponsible. His other-worldly sister—along with her mysteriously rich husband—produces the most destructive four-year-old child ever. All of Bagthorpe's children are talented but self-centered, except for poor Jack, the only member of the cast to possess an ounce of common sense. Cresswell's commission to re-edit E. Nesbit's classic fantasies inspired her to write *Return of the Psammead*, in which she carefully uses similar comic devices.

Alongside the Bagthorpe Saga Cresswell produced a series of fantasies, linked to the earlier novels by the allegory *The Winter of the Birds*. The theme of the mysterious hero in that book was given added psychological depth in *Dear Shrink* (that being the way the young hero addresses letters to famous psychiatrist Carl Jung). Three novels followed whose young heroines are distracted from their own personal losses by the necessity of saving

p.171

Artisans

Artisans are artists who produce useful products. A caterer can create cakes of exceptional beauty, making them almost an artistic object. Likewise, a furniture maker, a silversmith, or a glass blower concerned not just with the utility of the product he or she makes but also with the beauty of it can be referred to as an artisan. Artisan products are not usually mass produced.

Carl Jung

Carl Jung was a Swiss psychiatrist who collaborated with famous Austrian psychoanalyst Sigmund Freud beginning in 1907 to advance theories of psychoanalysis. By 1913, they had developed different ideas about psychoanalysis and went their separate ways. Jung believed that therapy was a way that people come in contact with their "collective unconcious." He contributed to the understanding of dreams, language, and the importance of myths and symbols.

children from past eras from awful fates: *The Secret World of Polly Flint*, *Moondial,* and *Stonestruck. Stonestruck*—which finds a heroic role for children evacuated to **Wales** from the East End of London during World War II— is the most powerful.

p.59

p.18

– Brian Stableford

Gillian Cross

Born: December 24, 1945; London, England

www.gillian-cross.co.uk

Gillian Cross is one of England's most admired writers of fiction for children and young adults. Her young adult books range from chilling stories of the supernatural to realistic thrillers. In all of them, protagonists are faced with the fact of evil and the necessity of making moral choices. p.233

Cross was born Gillian Clare Arnold and grew up in London, England. During her childhood, she often pretended that she was a famous author but did not begin writing fiction until she was in her late twenties. By then, she had bachelor's and master's degrees from Somerville College of Oxford University and a doctor of philosophy degree from the University of Sussex. While at Oxford, she married Martin Cross; the couple had four children. One night Cross realized that writing fiction would be much like inventing the stories she told her children. After three years of hard work, one of her books was finally accepted for publication. p.173

Sometimes Cross utilizes supernatural elements in her novels. In *The Dark Behind the Curtain*, spirits of the dead threaten the participants in a school play. It is up to two cast members, one of them the school rebel, to save the others from the ghosts.

Cross's realistic novels also pit her protagonists against forces of evil. In *On the Edge*, terrorists kidnap the protagonist, Tug Shakespeare, and it is up to a teenage girl to rescue him. Similarly, a terrorist is involved in *Wolf*. In *Phoning a Dead Man*, John Cox is hampered in his fight against Russian gangsters by the fact that he has lost his memory. Fortunately, his younger sister and his wheelchair-bound fiancé are determined to find him and bring him out of Siberia.

In other books, menacing forces at first appear to be merely psychological but ultimately prove to be real. In *Roscoe's Leap*, a twelve-year-old boy finds good reasons for his fear of the life-size **guillotine** in his house. In *Tightrope*, a fourteen-year-old girl p.174 thinks that her only worry is being found out as a nighttime graffiti artist until she realizes that she is the intended prey of a stalker and the pawn of a local hoodlum. One of the themes of Cross's works is the difficulty of discerning between illusion and reality. In *A Map of Nowhere*, Nick Miller discovers that what his brother's friends propose is not just a game, like his fantasy games, but a real crime. By contrast, in *Pictures in the Dark*, the protagonist finds that a desperate friend can indeed transform himself into an otter in order to defy a cruel father.

Oxford University

Oxford University is one of the best known and most respected universities in the world. It is also the oldest English-speaking university in the world. It is not known when Oxford was founded, but history shows that teaching has gone on there since 1096. The University is made up of 39 individual colleges. These were formed in academic halls or residences. All but one, now admit both men and women students. The relationship of the colleges to the university is similar to that of a state to the federal government. Each has defined responsibilites. Since each college could not provide facilities for all disciplines, such as scientific laboratories, the university provides them for the students.

Gillian Cross's skill in writing meaningful, suspenseful novels has brought her numerous honors, including the Carnegie Medal for *Wolf*. *On the Edge* was a runner-up for both the **Whitbread Children's Book of the Year** award and the **Edgar Award**. In 1992, one of Cross's many books for children, *The Great [American] Elephant Chase*, won the **Whitbread** award and the overall **Smarties Prize**.

p.42

– Rosemary M. Canfield Reisman

Guillotine

The guillotine is associated with the French Revolution, even though it existed long before as a tool for execution. The name came in 1789 when Dr. Guillotin submitted a proposition to the French Assembly that death should be by means of decapitation and without torture. In 1791, the Assembly agreed that any person condemned to the death penalty would have his head severed. In 1792, a guillotine was installed in Place du Carroussel in Paris. It was moved to the Place de la Révolution, now the Place de la Concorde, where King Louis XVI was executed in January, 1793, and the queen, Marie Antoinette, was executed in October of that year. The last public execution by guillotine took place in France in 1939, and the last execution by guillotine in the prison yard took place in 1977.

Chris Crutcher

Born: July 17, 1946; Dayton, Ohio

aboutcrutcher.com

Chris Crutcher has populated his novels with smart, funny, and ethical adolescents who are forced to make their way in a world populated by bigots, **homophobes**, and occasionally murderous adults. While a few of his characters, such as T. J. Jones, of *Whale Talk*, have wise and compassionate parents, most of his narrators and their friends are forced to seek wisdom and guidance outside their homes. Indeed, the father of *Staying Fat for Sarah Byrnes* and the stepfather in *Chinese Handcuffs* are pure evil, victimizing girls in ghastly and permanent ways.

p.10

263

The son of an Air Force pilot and a homemaker mother, Crutcher was born in Ohio and raised in Cascade, Idaho, a logging community north of Boise. Because his community was small and remote from the more varied opportunities of large cities, sports were of central importance. This interest shows up in Crutcher's novels, most of which take place in the Pacific Northwest, with athletes as their **protagonists**.

233

Crutcher himself knows how horrible life is for many children and adolescents. A former teacher, licensed therapist, and child-protection advocate, he has seen the aftermath of incest, torture, abandonment, neglect, rape, murder, and suicide. He

TITLES

Stotan!, 1986

Chinese Handcuffs, 1989

Athletic Shorts, 1991

Staying Fat for Sarah Byrnes, 1993

Ironman, 1995

Whale Talk, 2001

American Gladiators

American Gladiators was a television show from 1989 through 1996. It presented the professional "gladiators," beginning with three men and three women, who did battle against two male and two female challengers. The events tested strength, endurance, speed, and skill, involving everything from running up a downward moving conveyer belt, climbing a net wall, and dodging various foam rubber objects. The professionals were big, muscular men and women. The contestants were amateur athletes. The show developed almost cult-like fans.

addresses these problems in his fiction, not to court controversy and attention, but because they do occur and affect people's lives. Indeed, one of the dominant recurring themes in Crutcher's books is the need for people to take control of their own lives, confront the wrongs done to them, and move on in constructive ways. When Bo Brewster, of *Iron-man*, learns that his father is trying to ensure that he will lose a triathlon he is entering "for his own good," Bo's girlfriend Shelly repeats their anger-management teacher's admonition that people should stand up for themselves. With Shelly's encouragement, and that of his teachers, Bo harnesses his anger and competes successfully in the triathlon.

Shelly is enrolled in anger management and is training to become an **American Gladiator** in order to make constructive use of the rage that she feels for the abuse she received when she reported that her stepsister was being molested by a family member. Her family's violent rejection propelled her into self-destructive behavior until one civilized adult, her caseworker, stood up for her and suggested that she find ways to channel her energy into positive behaviors. In *Whale Talk*, T. J. Jones honors the dying wish of his murdered adoptive father by refusing to seek vengeance for that man's death.

p.45 A six-time winner of American Library Association book awards, Chris Crutcher received the American Library Association's Margaret A. Edwards Award. He also won the National Intellectual Freedom Award, given by the National Council of Teachers of English, in 1998.

.339

p.177

– Angela M. Salas

National Intellectual Freedom Award

The National Intellectual Freedom Award is granted each year by the National Council of Teachers of English. It honors an individual, group, or organization that has shown courage in advancing the cause of intellectual freedom or fighting censorship. It can be awarded for a single activity or for a series of ongoing events.

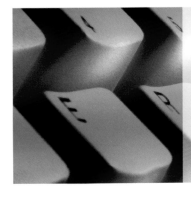

Karen Cushman

Born: October 4, 1941; Chicago, Illinois

www.scils.rutgers.edu/~kvander/cushman.html

Karen Cushman's books are known for their spirited female **protagonists** and intriguing historical settings. Her main characters are adolescent girls who initially have little control over their lives but learn to make the best of situations, allow others to help them, and even change their own circumstances when possible.

p.233

Although Cushman did not write her first book until she was in her fifties, her lifelong love of reading and her education helped prepare her for a writing career. After marrying and having a daughter, she went back to college to earn two master's degrees, including one in museum studies. This experience taught her how to research life in medieval England, the setting for which her novels are best known. Cushman's first book, *Catherine, Called Birdy*, took her more than three years to write but quickly earned critical praise and was named a **Newbery Honor Book**. Written as a diary, it tells the story of Catherine, the thirteen-year-old daughter of a minor medieval nobleman, who feels stifled by embroidery and the other "ladylike" tasks she is required to master. Defiant and alarmed by her father's attempts to marry her off, Catherine learns that while she may

p.10

not be able to control her own destiny, she can still affect her own happiness.

Cushman returned to a similar setting in her second book, *The Midwife's Apprentice*, but changed the point of view from a privileged person to one who is poverty stricken. A nameless orphan, burrowing in a dung heap for warmth, is relieved when she is taken on as an apprentice by a midwife. Alyce, as she eventually names herself, slowly realizes that she can make conscious decisions about her place in the world. Alyce's engaging personality and the book's frank portrayal of medieval poverty earned this book a **Newbery Medal**.

p.179

In contrast to Cushman's first two books, *The Ballad of Lucy Whipple* is set in the 1850's during the **California gold rush**. California Morning Whipple, who renames herself Lucy, is distressed when her recently widowed mother drags her and her siblings from Massachusetts to a rough California mining town. In *Rodzina*, Cushman draws upon her own Polish background to create a Polish orphan who is unwillingly placed on an orphan train traveling west from 1890's Chicago. As one of the older chil-

180

Midwifery

The practice of midwifery, assisting in childbirth, is an ancient one. Traditionally, childbirth occurred at home under the care of a midwife or family members. As medicine advanced, the role of the midwife was taken over by the doctor. Eventually, the place of childbirth was moved from the home into the hospital. By the 1920's, fewer babies in the U.S. were born at home than in the hospital. A movement developed among some midwives to combine their practice with that of a nurse, and the nurse-midwife was born. In 1955, the American College of Nurse Midwives was founded to accredit educational programs and provide professional standards. Meanwhile, those midwives whose training developed through experience continued to feel a need for their skills. In 1980, they formed the Midwives Alliance of North America (MANA), committed to the idea that childbirth should not take place in the clinical surroundings of the hospital but in the comfort of home.

dren, Rodzina is put in charge of several younger children during the long journey, a duty she initially resents. Both Lucy and Rodzina learn, however, that a family may be created in unexpected ways and places, and they are responsible for recognizing it. *The Ballad of Lucy Whipple* was adapted into a television movie in 2001.

In *Matilda Bone*, Cushman revisits medieval England but this time places her main character somewhere between nobility and poverty. Matilda is an orphan who has been raised and educated by priests but suddenly finds herself abandoned into the employ of Red Peg the Bonesetter. Matilda is horrified by her filthy surroundings and Peg's uneducated coarseness but she eventually recognizes the wisdom and compassion in those around her.

Karen Cushman's detailed and unromanticized historical settings give her books an unusual quality that many young adult readers enjoy. In addition, her memorable heroines are such that readers can simultaneously sympathize with and admire them.

— Amy Sisson

California Gold Rush

In January, 1848, gold was discovered at John Sutter's mill on the American River near Sacramento in California. Despite his attempts to keep the discovery quiet, word got out. By May, the rush had started. Men became scarce in the cities of California, as they rushed to the streams flowing from the Sierra Nevada. By August, a report appeared in the *New York Herald*. Soon gold seekers were filling ships sailing to California, and expeditions were traveling overland. By the end of 1849, the population of California had grown from fourteen thousand to more than one hundred thousand. This growth and attention helped to make the former Mexican province a state in 1850.

Paula Danziger

Born: August 18, 1944; Washington, D.C.
Died: July 8, 2004; New York, New York

www.scholastic.com/titles/paula

Paula Danziger wrote more than two dozen books for readers of all age groups. All the young adult novels that she wrote between 1974 and 1985 share a common theme: teenage girls in the midst of transformations and familial strife. Her later young adult novels share a common sense of adventure and have female protagonists who confront the world more openly than those in her earlier books. Danziger was one of the first writers to portray realistically the lives of modern teenagers, rather than sentimentalizing adolescence. Her interests were in the tough times that young adults face, as well as the ways they overcome their problems.

Born in Washington, D.C., and reared in Virginia, New Jersey, and other eastern States, Danziger always had an intense interest in books and writing. She often said that **John Ciardi**'s poetry and J. D. Salinger's novel *The Catcher in the Rye* (1951) influenced her reading and writing interests. She earned a bachelor's degree in English and became a middle school teacher and a counselor of junior high, high school, and college students. Two car accidents interrupted her academic career and forced her to find a different line of work, so she pursued a masters degree in writing and began to write stories based on her own life and the experiences of the students she had taught and counseled.

Danziger lived a life not unlike that of many of her female protagonists. Indeed, she modeled Marcy Lewis, the central character of *The Cat Ate My Gymsuit*, on herself. Danziger's parents did not get along

.233

.182

TITLES

The Cat Ate My Gymsuit, 1974

The Pistachio Prescription, 1978

Can You Sue Your Parents for Malpractice?, 1979

There's a Bat in Bunk Five, 1980

The Divorce Express, 1982

It's an Aardvark-Eat-Turtle World, 1985

This Place Has No Atmosphere, 1986

Remember Me to Harold Square, 1987

Thames Doesn't Rhyme with James, 1994

P.S. Longer Letter Later: A Novel in Letters, 1998 (with Ann M. Martin)

Snail Mail No More, 2000 (with Ann M. Martin)

John Ciardi

John Ciardi was a modern American poet who died in 1986. Unlike many poets, he felt poetry should be easy for the reader to understand. He also felt that poetry should have a positive effect on the reader. He recalled the origins of poetry and reminded readers that it should be read aloud, that its effect is to the ear not the eye. The subject of a poem, according to Ciardi, could be anything, and no words were banned from use. His poetry is true to his own creed in constructing a personality of its own.

well with each other, and she felt that they were unsupportive when she was a teenager. In the same way that she had to struggle to find herself, and like the process the students she mentored had to go through, her characters also go through transformative situations that are familiar to adolescents.

The Cat Ate My Gymsuit and its sequel, *There's a Bat in Bunk Five*, follow Marcy as she goes from being an outsider with a troubling home life to an outgoing young woman willing to challenge her school principal and actively pursue her interest in boys. *The Pistachio Prescription*, *Can You Sue Your Parents for Malpractice?*, *The Divorce Express*, and *It's an Aardvark-Eat-Turtle World*, the sequel to *The Divorce Express*, all share this same emphasis.

This Place Has No Atmosphere marks a stylistic change for Danziger. Its protagonist, Aurora is a teenager dealing with school and boys in a futuristic colony on the Moon. *Remember Me to Harold Square* and its sequel, *Thames Doesn't Rhyme with James*, follow the adventures of Kendra and her brother, Oscar, in New York City and London. In the same vein of stylistic difference, *P.S. Longer Letter Later* and its sequel, *Snail Mail No More*, both written with Ann M. Martin, are novels written in the form of letters. Danziger and Martin actually wrote the books by assuming the roles of their protagonists and writing letters to each other.

Because of Paula Danziger's ability to write stories that connect with children, teenagers, and adults, she received a number of writing awards, including a Parents' Choice Award, an **International Reading Association-Children's Book Council** Children's Choices Award, a **California Young Reader Medal**, and Hawaii's **Nene Award**. Danziger died of complications of a heart attack in 2004.

p.153

p.183

– Joshua Stein

Children's Choices

Each year publishers submit hundreds of books to the Children's Book Council. The books are distributed to hundreds of schools throughout the U.S. where children read the books and select the best 100 books. These book titles are compiled in an annotated list which is presented at the International Reading Association convention each year. The list is distributed to teachers, librarians, and parents to encourage reading of the best books of the year.

Ossie Davis

Born: December 18, 1917; Cogdell, Georgia

TITLE

Just Like Martin, 1992

Although actor **Ossie Davis** has written only one young adult novel, *Just Like Martin*, much of his drama speaks directly to youth. Regardless of his medium, Davis's consistent aim has been to portray the life and experience of African Americans as authentically as possible.

The son of a railroad construction worker and his wife, Davis left his native Georgia in 1935 to attend **Howard University** in Washington, D.C. Alain Locke, a well-known drama critic and professor of philosophy, encouraged his interest in theater. After leaving Howard in 1938, Davis worked at odd jobs as a shipping clerk, a janitor, and a stock clerk before he became associated with the McClendon Players in **Harlem**, mostly as a builder of sets rather than as an actor or playwright.

p.13

p.296

In 1942 Davis was drafted into the United States Army, in which he served throughout World War II as a medical technician. After his military discharge, he returned to Georgia. However, he was soon enticed to return to New York to rejoin the McClendon Players. In 1946 he played his first major role in *Jeb* and met another actor, Ruby Dee, whom he married two years later. Both went on to

Frederick Douglass

Frederick Douglass was born a slave in nineteenth century America. In 1838, he was able to escape from slavery. He then committed himself to work for the abolition of slavery so others could also be free. He became a popular speaker for antislavery societies and in 1845 published his *Narrative of the Life of Frederick Douglass: An American Slave*, one of the finest slave narratives. Douglass founded an abolitionist newspaper, became an Underground Railroad agent, wrote in support of women's rights, and revised his autobiography. During the Civil War, he urged the recruitment and equal treatment of blacks in the military. After the Civil War, he continued to speak out for racial equality until his death in 1895. He is remembered as the most prominent African American of his era.

distinguished acting careers on the stage and in films. In addition to his acting work, Davis has enjoyed a notable career as a playwright. First produced in 1961, his play *Purlie Victorious* later had a successful run on Broadway as *Purlie*. His biographical play *Escape to Freedom: A Play About Young Frederick Douglass* was performed in New York City's Town Hall in 1976 and won Davis both the **Coretta Scott King Book Award** and the **Jane Addams Children's Book Award**.

.185
.699
.668
.186
p.66
p.233

Just Like Martin focuses upon race relations in 1963, a critical year in the Civil Rights movement. Its protagonist, Isaac, nicknamed Stone, has a tense relationship with his father, Ike, who is grieving over the recent death of his wife, Stone's mother. He refuses to allow Stone, a straight-A high school student, to go with a group from his home in Alabama to participate in a civil rights demonstration and join the **March on Washington**, D.C. Ike fails to understand his son's devotion to nonviolence and his veneration of Martin Luther King, Jr. Stone hopes to become a preacher, "just like Martin."

The March on Washington

On August 28, 1963, more than 200,000 demonstrators marched through Washington, D.C., to encourage Congress to pass civil rights legislation and to celebrate the 100 year anniversary of the Emancipation Proclamation. One of the leaders of the march was Martin Luther King, Jr., whose historic "I Have a Dream" speech captivated the American public. While President John F. Kennedy would not live to see the civil rights bill passed, it became the top priority for President Lyndon Johnson, his former vice president. The following year saw the passage of the Civil Rights Act of 1964. The Reverend King, President Kennedy, and his younger brother Robert F. Kennedy—all passionate about civil rights legislation—were assassinated during this turbulent decade in American history.

After the meeting room in Stone's church is bombed, killing two of Stone's friends and seriously injuring another, Stone organizes a children's protest march. Stone's pastor questions whether Stone and his friends can remain nonviolent if they are attacked. However, Stone is convinced that this is possible. The upshot is that Ike slowly begins to accept and even embrace his son's values. The assassination of John F. Kennedy forces Ike to reevaluate his views of how to deal with the racial and social upheaval gripping the United States. The novel presents convincingly the development of the father-son relationship as Ike begins to learn from Stone and to espouse much of his outlook.

– R. Baird Shuman

Daniel Defoe

Born: 1660; London, England
Died: April 26, 1731; London, England
www.kirjasto.sci.fi/defoe.htm

Daniel Defoe is primarily known as the author of the novels *Robinson Crusoe* and *Moll Flanders*. However, he also wrote poetry, propaganda, travel guides, journalism, and other novels. In addition to his literary career, Defoe was a businessman, a political prisoner, and a spy. His family had been followers of Oliver Cromwell, but he was born in the same year that King Charles II was restored to the throne of England. He was a child during the calamitous years of 1665 and 1666, when London was ravaged by plague and fire. Although his family's religious beliefs prevented him from attending university, he was well educated at an academy run by the Reverend Charles Morton. There he was taught, among other things, how to argue a topic from all points of view—a skill that he put to good use in his journalistic career.

Defoe left school to go into business, trading hosiery, wine, and tobacco. In 1684 he married Mary Tuffey, with whom he had at least seven children. After a brief period of exile due to his participation in a rebellion against the Roman Catholic King James II in 1685, Defoe returned to business, only to go bankrupt in 1692. The time he spent in a **debtor's prison** acquainted him with the types of petty thieves and prostitutes

.188

TITLES

Robinson Crusoe, 1719

The Farther Adventures of Robinson Crusoe, 1719

Moll Flanders, 1722

who people his novels, particularly *Moll Flanders*. On being released from prison, Defoe once again went into business. This time he got into trouble as a result of his political and religious beliefs. However, he was offered a shortcut out of prison: He was to become a journalist promoting the pro-Anglican Tory party line. When the Tory government fell in 1714, p.189 Defoe was conscripted by the Whigs to work as their agent, undermining the Tory paper *The Weekly Journal* from within. He continued this spy game for almost a decade, until his double-dealing was discovered by his publisher. The last half dozen or so years of his life he spent as he had the rest of them: writing and avoiding his creditors.

Defoe wrote his novels in the midst of this tumultuous activity, inspired by current events and his own experiences. *Robinson Crusoe* is the tale of a man shipwrecked on an unidentified Caribbean island who must learn to become self-sufficient. He inhabits something approaching a solitary Utopia, or perfect land, for twenty-four years, until the arrival of cannibals. His saving of their intended victim, a man whom he names Friday, leads to his contact with the outside world and eventual return to England.

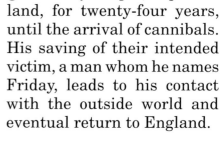

Debtor's Prison

People who did not pay the money owed to others for goods or services rendered were often thrown into debtor's prison. This practice occurred in both Britain and the United States. The individual had to pay the debts and also was charged for room and board for the period of time in prison. It is no longer common practice to put people in jail for not paying their debts.

Tories and Whigs

These two British political parties have a long history. In Defoe's time, Tory applied to the group who defended the monarchy and the inherited right to the crown. This party represented the land owners. The Whigs were the party of the new finance and merchant classes. In the nineteenth century, the Tories became the Conservative Party and the Whigs the Liberal Party.

Moll Flanders is a decidedly racier tale than *Crusoe*, recounting the adventures of a woman who careens through all levels of society on both sides of the Atlantic, as a servant, a prostitute, a petty thief, a wife, a mistress, a mother, and an unwitting committer of incest. There is a certain irony, intentional or not, in the fact that Moll's story is told as a tale of repentance for her former sinful ways, yet Moll survives, and even flourishes, despite it all.

– Leslie Ellen Jones

Walter de la Mare

Born: April 25, 1873; Charlton, England
Died: June 22, 1956; Twickenham, England

www.bluetree.co.uk/wdlmsociety/contents.htm

TITLES

Henry Brocken, 1904

The Turnip, 1927

The Wind Blows Over, 1936

The Collected Tales of Walter de la Mare, 1950

Although known primarily as a poet and writer of childhood tales, **Walter de la Mare** also wrote stories dealing with the supernatural and the paranormal that appeal to young adult readers. Often set in strange lands or exotic locations, these stories are enticing and mysterious. In some of his tales, the protagonists are adolescents, or children with precocious awareness of the unusual or atypical. De la Mare's language is rooted in the syntax and style of Victorian England. It may seem difficult to modern American readers; however, it may also recall the rhythms and descriptive passages of the traditional nursery rhymes gathered in Mother Goose collections.

p.233

p.572

Born Walter John Delamare in a London suburb, de la Mare (who later adopted the original French spelling of his family name) was the sixth of seven children. His father, who was sixty-one when de la Mare was born, worked at the Bank of England. His mother was twenty-two years younger. A distant relative of the poet Robert Browning, his mother brought to the family a serious interest in literature from her well-educated Scots father.

p.191

At the age of fourteen, de la Mare became editor of the St. Paul's *Chorister Journal*, his school news-

Robert Browning

Robert Browning is well known for his romanticized marriage to Elizabeth Barrett. In 1845, Browning sent her a letter for the first time, complimenting the internationally-known Barrett on a volume of poems she had written. A correspondence began, and he became a frequent visitor at her home in London. She was a thirty-nine-year-old invalid, and he was a thirty-two-year-old poet and playwright. Elizabeth's father forbade any of his children from marrying, so Robert and she conducted their courtship in secret. In 1846, they secretly married and left for Europe. Her father refused to ever see Elizabeth again. The Brownings settled in Florence, Italy, living in the Casa Guidi. They both continued to publish poetry, for which they are among the best-known of the Victorian English poets.

paper, which he wrote almost single-handedly. After graduation, he became a bookkeeper for the Anglo-American Oil Company. Although he did no writing for publication at that time, he was composing skits and charades for a local dramatic club. In 1895 he and a few friends started a journal of stories and light verse. After several rejections, his first story, "Kismet" was published that same year. By the next year, he was composing booklets of poetry for his nephews and nieces. Some of these were the first versions of poems that would later be among his best-known works.

De la Mare is remembered as a writer who could evoke and convey the spirit of childhood's realm with exquisite style, but he was also interested in imaginative excursions into regions beyond the literal reality of Edwardian England. *Henry Brocken* is a novel that follows a young man through a *Wanderjahr*—or, possibly, a daydream voyage—in which he meets various literary characters, including Jane

Companion of Honor

In the United Kingdom, honors are awarded twice a year. Most are made in the Order of the British Empire. They are awarded to those in public service, in the arts, in sports, in industry and trade unions, in science, in journalism, in diplomatic service, in the armed services, and those providing volunteer service to their communities. Individuals can be nominated by anyone. The list of honors is published in the *London Gazette* and national newspapers. Recipients are invited to Buckingham Palace in London, the Palace of Holyrood House in Edinburgh, or regional locations to receive their award from the Queen or other senior member of the royal family.

Eyre, Lemuel Gulliver, and Annabelle Lee. *The Turnip*, which de la Mare adapted from a story by the Brothers Grimm, seems like a child's morality tale. However, some of its language, imagery, and social commentary makes it appropriate for older readers as well.

The Wind Blows Over, and the larger volume, *The Collected Tales of Walter de la Mare*, include stories in which characters seem caught in a condition of stasis or transition between the natural and supernatural worlds. They often depict young people as outsiders not fully accepted in adult society.

p.192 Walter De la Mare was widely admired and honored in the latter decades of his life. In 1948 he was made a **Companion of Honor** of the British Empire by King George VI. After he died, he was buried in St. Paul's Cathedral in London, among other prominent Englishman.

– Leon Lewis

Sarah Dessen

Born: June 6, 1970; Evanston, Illinois

www.sarahdessen.com

Sarah Dessen writes honest, witty books about teenage girls who live in the suburbs. Her p.233 protagonists worry about such things as being popular; becoming independent of their mothers; and boyfriends who push them toward drugs, insist on sexual intimacy, and even descend to physical abuse.

Born in Illinois, Dessen later moved to Chapel Hill, North Carolina, where her father was an English professor. She was always surrounded by books and encouraged to read, especially by her mother, who liked books with strong female characters. Dessen started writing when she was still young. As a shy child, she also soon discovered the value of friendship. Her friends and family helped her through adolescence, when she felt unattractive and insecure—much like some of the heroines of her later books.

After high school, Dessen entered the **University of North Carolina at Chapel** p.194 **Hill**, majoring in creative writing. In 1993 she received a bachelor's degree with highest honors. However, she kept working as a waitress so that she could spend her afternoons writing. Her always supportive parents were not surprised when she published her first book only three years after graduation. The following year, she became a lecturer at the University of North Carolina in Chapel Hill, where she continued to live and to write.

TITLES

That Summer, 1996

Someone Like You, 1998

Keeping the Moon, 1999

Dreamland, 2000

This Lullaby, 2002

The Truth About Forever, 2004

The protagonist of Dessen's first novel, *That Summer*, is Haven, a tall, awkward, fifteen-year-old girl whose older sister Ashley is about to be married. Haven explains in no uncertain terms why she detests her sister's fiancé, her new stepmother, the woman friend her mother has acquired, and even the sister who was once so close to her. It takes one of Ashley's discarded boyfriends to convince Haven that she is an attractive young woman, thus defusing her rage.

Someone Like You also has a first-person narrator, sixteen-year-old Halley. Although her comments about life at school, at home, and at the mall are often funny, Halley and her best friend, Scarlett, both have serious problems. The boy whom Halley loves is pressuring her to have sex, and Scarlett's boyfriend has been killed, leaving her pregnant. Both girls find strength in their mutual friendship and in their supportive families. Friendship is also the theme of Dessen's third book, *Keeping the Moon*, in which new friends combine to give Colie Sparks a makeover and, more important, to convince her of

University of North Carolina at Chapel Hill

The University of North Carolina at Chapel Hill is one of the oldest universities in the U.S. Chartered in 1789, it first opened its doors to students in 1795. One of the few Southern universities to remain open during the Civil War, it was closed during Reconstruction from 1870 to 1875. It had always been funded by fees and donations, but in 1881, the school began receiving money from the state. In 1897, the university enrolled its first female student. By 1995, some 23,000 students were enrolled, and the faculty totaled some 2,200 members. Since its founding, more than 780,000 students have been educated at the university.

School Library Journal

Founded in 1954, *SLJ* is a professional magazine published by Reed Business Information. It is written for librarians working at schools and public libraries serving young readers. It features articles on technology and other issues that librarians need to know about. It also features reviews of books that librarians may want to consider adding to the library collection.

her real worth. Dessen never suggests that there are easy answers for life's problems. In *Dreamland*, Caitlin O'Koren is so badly abused by her boyfriend that she is institutionalized, and the heroine of *This Lullaby* is only too aware of the fact that her romance with a rock musician may not end happily.

Perhaps more than any other quality, it is Sarah Dessen's honesty that makes her popular with young adult readers. *That Summer, Someone Like You*, and *Keeping the Moon* were all named **Best Books for Young Adults** by the American Library Association, and *School Library Journal* chose *Keeping the Moon* as a **Best Book of the Year**.

p.480
p.45
p.195

– Rosemary M. Canfield Reisman

Charles Dickens

Born: February 7, 1812; Portsmouth, Hampshire, England

Died: June 9, 1870; Gad's Hill, near Rochester, Kent, England

www.victorianweb.org/authors/dickens/dickensov.html

Although modern teachers would like young adults to read **Charles Dickens** primarily because he is long dead and highly respected, his work is far more interesting to adolescent readers than such reasons might imply. It includes—among much else—all the key elements of modern young adult fiction.

A key to the novels of Dickens is a reversal of fortune that he personally experienced at the age of twelve His father, a clerk in the Royal Navy's pay office at Chatham, England, was **imprisoned for debt**, and Dickens himself was sent to work in a p.188 blacking factory. The disgrace and hardship were temporary, but the experience would make a deep impression on his future books. His work exhibits a keen sense of how traumas experienced in childhood can threaten an entire lifetime with frustrated hopes.

Although the notion of writing books specifically for "young adults" was unknown in Dickens's day, Dickens was enthusiastic, both as a writer and as editor of the periodicals *Household Words* and *All the Year Round*, to address his work to readers of all ages. The only one of his novels to feature a protagonist who remains a child throughout the entire p.233 story is *Oliver Twist*, but Dickens's other apparently-biographical novels pay careful attention to the years of adolescence. *Nicholas Nickleby*, *David Copperfield*, and *Hard Times* include some of the earliest literary accounts of English school life, while *David Copperfield* and *Great Expectations* offer painstak-

Serial Publication

Charles Dickens published most of his works first in weekly periodicals. He would publish one chapter in each weekly issue, then turn all of the chapters into a published book at the end. This is an extremely demanding way to write a book and puts a lot of pressure on the author. The publication of *Bleak House*, for example, went on for a period of a year and a half.

ing accounts of adult lives shadowed, shaped and brought to the brink of ruin by events that happen in the main characters' adolescent years. *The Old Curiosity Shop* is a classic **melodrama** that taught future generations of writers how to get the greatest possible reader response from the tragedy of a child forced to grow old before her time and finally be destroyed by too much responsibility.

p.198

The cast of memorable minor characters in Dickens's novels includes many different adolescent types. The Artful Dodger in *Oliver Twist*, Dick Swiveller in *The Old Curiosity Shop* and Steerforth in *David Copperfield* are manipulative and ambitious. They are more memorable than his depictions of such victims as Smike in *Nicholas Nickleby* or such would-be heroes as Kit Nubbles in *The Old Curiosity Shop*, not only because of the anger they arouse in readers but because of the attention paid to how they became such bad characters.

Charles Dickens became an opponent of teachers who wanted children's literature to be realistic. As an **editor** he established the Christmas supplement as a place to publish for recreational and fanciful fiction. Moreover, his own Christmas stories helped lay the foundations for mod-

p.20

ern supernatural fiction. *A Christmas Carol*, for example, is more remarkable for its account of how Ebenezer Scrooge became such a miserly character during Christmases past than for his eventual change of heart. *The Chimes*—which Dickens intended to strike "a great blow" on behalf of the disadvantaged by attacking the popular Victorian p.572 distinction drawn between the "deserving" and "undeserving" poor—will rally young readers against injustice.

– Brian Stableford

Melodrama

A melodrama is a dramatic work with exaggerated theatrics, a detailed plot, much physical action, but little character development. It originated in France shortly before 1800 and became popular in England shortly thereafter. It was often a more popular form of theater than serious tragedy or comedy. During the twentieth century, theatergoers began to prefer realism. Today, the influence of melodrama can be seen in the use of music to reinforce emotional moments in drama and in the skill of set designers and builders to achieve visual effects.

Peter Dickinson

Born: December 16, 1927; Livingstone, Northern
Rhodesia (now Zambia)

www.peterdickinson.com

Although **Peter Dickinson** can write brilliantly in a light spirit, as in the mock-nonfictional *The Flight of Dragons* and such quirky fantasies for younger children as *A Box of Nothing* (1985), he is particularly distinguished as a writer of earnest, challenging, and thought-provoking fiction for young adults.

Born in Central Africa and educated at **Eton** and **King's College, Cambridge**, England, Dickinson served in the British army for three years before embarking on a career in journalism. He worked on the humor magazine *Punch* from 1952 until 1969, quitting when he achieved immediate success as a writer of crime fiction and young adult fiction. His first young adult novel, *The Weathermonger*, is an English postcatastrophe story, in which the influence of a drug-addled wizard Merlin prohibits the use of technology. Its superior "prequels," *Heartsease* and *The Devil's Children*, which complete the Changes trilogy, describe the painful adaptation of British society to this reversal of the **Industrial Revolution**. Dickinson's subsequent work for young adults retains a strong interest in the consequences of power that is misused.

This theme is explored in psychological thrillers such as *The Gift*, in which an adolescent **telepath** comes into contact with a dangerous **psychopath**, and *Healer*, in which a girl with healing powers becomes the instrument of an exploitative institution. The theme's political projections are featured in three fine **historical novels**: *The Blue Hawk*, set in

.200

p.5

.531

.444

.707

p.117

TITLES

The Weathermonger, 1968

Heartsease, 1969

The Devil's Children, 1970

Emma Tupper's Diary, 1971

The Dancing Bear, 1972

The Gift, 1973

Chance, Luck, and Destiny, 1975

The Blue Hawk, 1976

Annerton Pit, 1977

The Flight of Dragons, 1979

Tulku, 1979

The Seventh Raven, 1981

Healer, 1983

Eva, 1988

AK, 1990

A Bone from a Dry Sea, 1992

Shadow of a Hero, 1994

The Kin, 1998 (publ. in the United States in 4 volumes: *Suth, Noll, Po,* and *Mana*)

Touch and Go, 1997

The Lion Tamer's Daughter, 1999

The Ropemaker, 2001

The Tears of the Salamander, 2003

p.44

ancient Egypt; *The Dancing Bear*, set in sixth century **Byzantium**; and *Tulku*, set at the time of China's early twentieth century Boxer Rebellion. The second and third novels describe difficult educational journeys, as does the grimly realistic *AK*, whose hero is a child soldier in a strife-riven modern African nation.

Dickinson's hostage drama, *The Seventh Raven*, also carries the themes of political corruption and desperation into a modern context. The fine science-fiction novel *Eva* similarly combines the personal and the political in the heart-rending story of a young girl injured in a road accident who, through technology, is "reincarnated" in the body of a chimpanzee. She becomes responsible for the return of her threatened species to the wild.

Dickinson carried forward environmentalist concerns from his Changes trilogy. The mildly satirical *Emma Tupper's Diary* and the thriller *Annerton Pit* are extended in *Eva* into a meditation on human nature. This thought is further expanded in the two story lines of *A Bone from a Dry Sea*, which contrasts the explorations of **paleontologists** in modern Africa with an account of early human existence, and *The Kin*, an elaborate reconstruction of the origins of *Homo sapiens* through the lives of four adolescents. These novels are Dickinson's greatest literary

p.201

Eton College

Eton is a private British high school that now admits about 1,300 boys ages 13 through 18 for study. It is a boarding school, so all of the boys live in dormitories on the school grounds. It was founded by King Henry VI in 1440 and is located about twenty miles west of London on the River Thames. It is a very prestigous school and many important Britons have attended Eton. Students still dress in an old-fashioned school uniform.

Paleontology

Paleontology is the study of fossils, the physical remnants of former life. Since more than 99 percent of all species that have ever existed are now extinct, fossils provide our only record of evolution. Fossils are incomplete, so it is difficult to create an exact record. Many lines of evolution can be traced through time when used with relative and scientific dating methods.

p.87

achievements to date. The off-beat quest fantasy *The Rope-maker* revisits the concerns of the Changes trilogy in a setting carefully designed to achieve that purpose.

p.42

Peter Dickinson's many writing awards include prestigious **Carnegie Medals** for *Tulku* and *City of Gold*, **Whitbread Children's Book of the Year** honors for *Tulku* and *AK*, the **Michael L. Printz Honor Book** award for *The Ropemaker*, and the

p.488

.747

Boston Globe-Horn Honor Book award for *Eva*.

– Brian Stableford

Berlie Doherty

Born: November 6, 1943; Liverpool, England

www.berliedoherty.com

Berlie Doherty writes realistic novels about issues that young adults confront in their lives and care about deeply. Much of the power of her prose, in fact, comes from her ability to connect with her readers. Moreover, her prose is elegant and sophisticated, oftentimes narrating a story from multiple perspectives.

The youngest of three children, Doherty always liked writing. Her father encouraged her early attempts, sending them to newspapers where they were published on children's pages. However, at fourteen, she seemed too old to publish on those pages, and her writing career stalled. After graduating from the University of Durham in 1965 with a degree in English, she worked as a social worker, teacher, and radio broadcaster for the **British Broadcasting Corporation** (BBC). She married and had three children. While taking a creative-writing class in 1978, Doherty began writing again. One of her stories was bought by the BBC and produced as a **radio play**. Doherty might have had a late start as a professional writer, but it was impressive. By 1983, after publishing her first novel, she was a full-time writer and a now single mother supporting three children.

Not surprisingly, perhaps, Doherty often portrays family life in her books. Both *White Peak Farm*

p.6

p.564

and *Granny Was a Buffer Girl* focus on the closeness among family members. In the first book, family members' stories create a portrait of life on an English farm. In the second book, family members reveal details about their lives before Jess's departure abroad. Focusing on teenage pregnancy in her most popular novel, *Dear Nobody*, Doherty shows how pregnancy changes the lives not only of Chris and Helen, the couple involved, but also the lives of their families.

Street Child illustrates the difficulties of life without family. Focusing on an orphan named Jim Jarvis, *Street Child* is based on the true story of **Doctor Barnardo** and the children's refuge he created in the 1860's. *The Snake-Stone* focuses on adoption as James Logan, a diving champion with loving adoptive parents, becomes obsessed with finding his birth mother. What he learns, just as Jim Jarvis does, is that family may have little relation to biological connections. Doherty's

Barnardo's

Thomas Barnardo was an entrepenuerial Victorian who established a network of homes for homeless children. At his death in 1905, there were ninety-six Barnardo's homes caring for more than 8,500 children. More children were placed with families, and a great number were sent to Canada and Australia. As society changed so did the ideas of how to treat homeless, orphaned, or abused children. The attitude that children needed a normal home life replaced that of putting children in group homes. In 1966, Dr. Barnardo's Homes became simply Dr. Barnardo's, the residential service was ended, and focus was shifted to emotional and behavioral problems. Since 1988, the charity is simply named Barnardo's and it continues to work with children and families. It also assists with foster care and adoption.

Daughter of the Sea is, in a sense, an adoption story as well. A retelling of the Selkie folk tale, this novel depicts a fisherman raising a human daughter descended from seals. Family for the protagonist in p.233 *Holly Starcross*, becomes difficult when Holly's father, absent for eight years, reappears in her life.

Among other honors, Berlie Doherty captured Great Britain's prestigious **Carnegie Medal** for p.4 *Granny Was a Buffer Girl* and *Dear Nobody*. Six of her other novels have also been nominated for the Carnegie award. In 2002 she received an **honorary** p.204 **doctorate** from the University of Derbyshire for her work. In addition to writing young adult books, she is the author of books for children and adults. Doherty has published more than forty books, several of which have been translated into other languages or adapted to film, television, or the stage.

– Cassandra Kircher

Honorary Doctorate

Universities often select noteworthy individuals to receive an honorary doctorate degree. The recipient of this degree does not attend classes or write a dissertation. Instead, he or she is recognized and distinguished as an outstanding person who has contributed to his or her field. The degree also can be awarded to someone who has made significant financial donations to the institution. The individual is entitled to add the Dr. title before his or her name.

Michael Dorris

Born: January 30, 1945; Louisville, Kentucky
Died: April 11, 1997; Concord, New Hampshire
www.ipl.org/div/natam/bin/browse.pl/A32

Although **Michael Dorris** is best known for his adult novels and his nonfiction book *The Broken Cord* (1989), he also wrote four memorable novels geared toward young adult audiences. These books portray young Native Americans dealing with issues of self-identity, the coming of age, and family. The characters in all four books are complicated humans beings, not the Indian stereotypes often portrayed in popular books and films.

Dorris's own heritage was mixed. His father was a Native American; his mother was part French and part Irish. In various ways, his life and his career were heavily influenced by racial identity—especially by his Native American roots. Dorris spent part of his youth growing up on an **Indian reservation** and was devoted to Native American causes, including more respectful study and depictions of Native Americans in public education. In 1972 he founded the **Native American Studies** program at Dartmouth College, where he was a professor—intermittently—for twenty-five years.

In his mid-twenties, Dorris became one of the first single men in the United States to adopt a child legally. His son, Adam, a Native American diagnosed with fetal alcohol syndrome, became the subject of Dorris's award-winning *The Broken Cord*, a book that helped inspire legislation requiring that women be informed of the dangers of drinking alcohol while they are pregnant. When Dorris married Louise Erdrich in 1981, he became connected with someone very much like him: a writer who was part

p.725

.206

.207

TITLES

Morning Girl, 1992

Guests, 1994

Sees Behind Trees, 1996

The Window, 1997

Native American and who focused on Native American themes in her work. Together he and Louise raised six children: three of their own and three of Native American heritage whom they adopted.

It was not until after the death of Adam in 1991 that Dorris began writing books for young adults. The first three of his books are historical, set in the p.11 fifteenth and sixteenth centuries. *Morning Girl*, for example, unfolds on an uninhabited Caribbean island in 1492. It depicts a young girl, Morning Girl, and her brother, Evening Star, playing and fighting together in the months before the Italian explorer Christopher Columbus arrives at the book's end and bring changes that will destroy the islanders' way of life. This book won the Scott O'Dell Award for Historical Fiction.

p.51

Dorris's second novel, *Guests*, also focuses on interactions between Native American and non-Native American peoples. Its protagonist, p.233 a young Native American named Moss, is angered that his people have invited European outsiders to his village for a Thanksgiving-like celebration. In *Sees Behind Trees*, Walnut, a

young Native American with poor eyesight, learns to "see" in other ways and is thus able to lead his grandfather to the land of water. Young readers of all backgrounds relate easily to Dorris's protagonists, whose lives are simultaneously different from and similar to their own.

Unlike the young adult novels that preceded it, *The Window*, with its modern setting, chronicles the early life of Rayona, a young person of both African and Native American heritage, who first appears as a teenager in Dorris's *A Yellow Raft in Blue Water* (1987) and later as an adult in *Cloud Chamber* (1997). Dorris, who suffered from chronic depression and who had numerous personal problems, took his own life in April, 1997.

– Cassandra Kircher

Fetal Alcohol Syndrome

When a mother consumes alcohol during pregnancy, it can result in retarded growth and mental or physical problems in the child. This disorder was first identified in the early 1970's. The damage can be subtle or severe and depends on the amount of alcohol consumed and when. Early pregnancy is a particularly critical period, both developmentally for the fetus and because the woman may not know she is pregnant. Because it is not known how much alcohol can cause problems, it is best for women not to drink when pregnant or planning a pregnancy.

Arthur Conan Doyle

Born: May 22, 1859; Edinburgh, Scotland
Died: July 7, 1930; Crowborough, England
www.sherlockholmesonline.org

TITLES

Arthur Conan Doyle is most famous as the creator of Sherlock Holmes, the private detective par excellence. However, his literary output was vast and also included stories of action, adventure, and lost worlds.

Doyle's father, an Irishman who was a civil servant in Edinburgh, Scotland, traveled in an artistic and literary circle that left a strong mark on his son. After schooling in England and Austria, Doyle returned to Edinburgh in 1876 to study medicine at the university. There he met Joseph Bell, an instructor of extraordinary deductive skills. Bell was to provide the inspiration for Doyle's most enduring literary character. By 1879 Doyle had begun his literary career. However, the next year he signed on as ship's surgeon on a whaler headed to the Arctic. Returning to Edinburgh only to take his final exams for his bachelor of medicine degree, he next signed on as the doctor on a freight ship bound for Africa. When he returned to Britain, he ended up practicing medicine in Southsea, England, and found himself making more money from his occasional short-story writing than from his medical work. In 1885 he received his doctor of medicine degree from Edinburgh and married Louise Hawkins, the sister of one of his patients. The necessity of providing for a wife forced Doyle to make some decisions about his career. He decided that he had a better chance of success as a writer than as a doctor.

Doyle decided that if he were to develop a base of readers, he needed to create an ongoing character,

221b Baker Street

The fictional home of Sherlock Holmes and Dr. Watson from 1881 to 1904 was at 221b Baker Street in London, England. The building at this address, which was last used as a boarding house until 1936, is now open to the public as the Sherlock Holmes Museum. The first floor study overlooking Baker Street has been maintained as it was in Victorian times.

and one whose adventures could be self-contained, so that his readers would not have to read long stories in monthly installments and be disappointed if they missed chapters. Inspired by Edgar Allan Poe's fictional detective M. Dupin and Émile Gaboriau's Lecoq, Doyle decided to try his hand at detective fiction. The result was Sherlock Holmes—a fictionalized version of his old medical teacher Joseph Bell. The hallmark of his detective was Holmes's brilliance at deducing facts from the most subtle and unlikely types of evidence. Doyle's first Holmes books were an immense success; however, he soon began to feel constrained by his creation. Plots of sufficient complexity for Holmes to solve were difficult to construct. He tried to kill Holmes off in "The Final Solution" by sending the detective over the Reichenbach Falls, but the outrage of his readership forced him to resurrect his hero.

In his later life, Doyle became known as an advocate of spiritualism, the belief that one can communicate with the dead, and he was also

The Cottingley Fairy Photos

Photos taken by sixteen-year-old Elsie Wright and her ten-year-old cousin Francis Griffiths in their Yorkshire garden using Elsie's cutout fairies resulted in a national controversy. Were these small, winged fairies real? A 1997 film, *Fairy Tale, A True Story*, recreates the sensation in 1917 England.

outspoken in his support of the so-called **Cottingley Fairy photographs**. This school-girl hoax caused a commotion in 1917 when many people accepted the pictures as proof of a world of tiny fairies unseen by human eyes.

p.210

Arthur Conan Doyle's popularity as a writer lies in his mixture of science and magic. Sherlock Holmes's deductions are so precise and insightful that his associate Dr. Watson regards them as something approaching **sorcery**. However, Holmes is always able to explain his deductions with only the facts that are before him. It is his powers of observation that are extraordinary, and readers may infer that any person who adopts Holmes's methods might match his brilliance as a detective. Doyle gave the final impetus to the formation of the detective story genre, a genre better known as "mystery," a term that originally referred to the secret doctrines of a religion or a craft, and in his hands, that tension between reason and the supernatural was never completely resolved.

p.551

– Leslie Ellen Jones

Daphne du Maurier

Born: May 13, 1907; London, England
Died: April 19, 1989; Par, Cornwall, England

www.dumaurier.org

Best known for her novel *Rebecca*, **Daphne du Maurier** was most popular during the 1940's and 1950's. She left a legacy of interesting novels, several of which are of particular interest to young adult readers. Many of her novels are psychological thrillers, horror and suspense stories, or historical romances featuring well-formed and colorful characters who are often destroyed by their own intense passions and plots that often end without clear resolutions.

Du Maurier was born in London, England, and lived an unusually privileged life. Her paternal grandfather was **George du Maurier**, an author who may have been Daphne du Maurier's greatest inspiration. Her father, Gerald du Maurier, was a successful actor. Daphne du Maurier published her first novel, *The Loving Spirit*, in 1931. The success of her first book brought her to the attention of Fredrick Browning, a Grenadier Guard whom she married in 1932.

Du Maurier's most important novel, *Rebecca*, is the story of an insecure young woman who marries a widower many years her senior and suddenly finds herself transported into a life of privilege living in an old English

p.117

212

TITLES

Jamaica Inn, 1936

Rebecca, 1938

The House on the Strand, 1969

Echoes from the Macabre, 1976

Classics from the Macabre, 1987

estate called Manderley. The story is told from the young woman's point of view as she faces the demons of the memory of her husband's first wife, Rebecca. While she is living in the grand house over which Rebecca had been mistress, she makes many excruciatingly painful blunders—all under the watchful eyes of the servants, who detest her for trying to take the place of the previous Mrs. de Winter.

Jamaica Inn, which du Maurier wrote two years before *Rebecca*, is the story of another young woman, Mary Yellan, who travels to live with her aunt after the death of her mother. Upon joining her aunt she encounters her brutal Uncle Joss Merlyn and becomes trapped in the treachery and evil that surrounds her. In *The House on the Strand*, a young man experimenting with hallucinogenic drugs finds himself able to move back and forth between the present day and the fourteenth century in Cornwall. Each additional experiment with the drug that he makes leads him to question the monotonous life he leads in reality, while inextricably moving him toward great perils.

Other excellent du Maurier works that young adult readers enjoy include her collections of horror and suspense stories, *Echoes from the Macabre* and *Classics from the Macabre*. Her short story "The Birds," which is included in both of those volumes, is an excellent example of her liking for gruesome sto-

George du Maurier

Born in Paris of a French father and English mother, du Maurier became an English novelist and illustrator. Calling on his youthful experiences in artistic Paris, du Maurier created the romantic bohemian setting of Paris in his novel *Trilby*. While entertaining, it is not a great work of literature, but it did give us the classic character of Svengali. The man of strange powers possesses the title character, Trilby, and only through alliance with him does she become a successful singer. The name now has the dictionary definition "one who attempts with evil intentions to persuade or force another to do his bidding."

Alfred Hitchcock

Alfred Hitchcock is one of the best known and most respected movie directors in the history of film. He is often referred to as the "Master of Suspense," but he was actually much more. He filmed versions of three of Daphne du Maurier's works: *Jamaica Inn*, *Rebecca*, and "The Birds." *Jamaica Inn*, his last film in England, was a flop. However, his first American movie, *Rebecca*, was a success, winning the Academy Award for Best Picture in 1940. In his 1963 film *The Birds*, he successfully captured du Maurier's shocking short story of birds gone murderous, moving it to contemporary time and placing it in the San Francisco area.

ries. In this story, Mother Nature goes terribly awry when ordinary English birds suddenly become murderous.

Both *Rebecca* and "The Birds" were made into classic movies by the legendary filmmaker Alfred Hitchcock, who appreciated du Maurier's ability to create a terrifying and suspenseful story. Daphne du Maurier's work is considered an excellent gateway for young adults to begin to explore the world of adult fiction.

p.213

– Grace Jasmine

Lois Duncan

Born: April 28, 1934; Philadelphia, Pennsylvania

http://loisduncan.arquettes.com/lois3.html

Lois Duncan is well known for her ability to place seemingly ordinary teenage characters in extraordinary and dangerous situations without sacrificing believability. Her teenagers are usually the first to notice when sinister things begin happening, while adults are slow to take their warnings seriously. While only some of Duncan's plots contain supernatural elements, virtually all her books feature characters who must find inner strength to solve their own problems.

Born Lois Duncan Steinmetz, Duncan began writing magazine stories before she was thirteen and eventually graduated to novel-length works. Her earliest publications were mainstream love stories, but it was not until she published *Ransom*, a suspense novel in which five teenagers are kidnapped by a school bus driver, that her work began receiving more popular and critical attention. Duncan then realized that she had a talent for writing young adult suspense fiction. She followed *Ransom* with *They Never Came Home*, in which two boys mysteriously disappear on a camping trip, and *I Know What You Did Last Summer*, in which a group of teenagers who share a grim secret are terrorized.

After these successes, Duncan began incorporating supernatural elements into her plots. In *Down a Dark Hall*, Kit is sent to an exclusive **boarding school** whose entire student body consists of four students, each of whom possesses an **extrasensory ability**. Duncan's next several books alternated between supernatural and realistic suspense, including *Summer of Fear*, in which a summer visitor turns out to be a malevolent witch; *Killing Mr. Griffin*, in which a group prank to kidnap a teacher turns deadly; and *The Twisted Window*, in which a teenager named Tracy becomes enmeshed in a domestic kidnapping dispute. Her later titles contained more imaginative supernatural elements. In *Stranger with My Face*, for example, the adopted Laurie learns that her long-lost twin sister wants to possess her body using astral projection. In *The Third Eye*, a girl reluctantly accepts the burden of her psychic abilities, while *Locked in Time* features a young girl who suspects that her suspiciously young new stepmother has a dangerous secret.

p.168
306

Duncan's most chilling book, however, is not supernatural fiction. It is a work of nonfiction that was named an **American Library Association** Best Book for Young Adults even though it was originally written for adults. Titled *Who Killed My Daughter?* (1992), this book chronicles the unsolved murder of Duncan's youngest daughter, **Kaitlyn**, who was eighteen at the time of her death in 1989. Duncan noted that the circumstances of

p.45
480
216

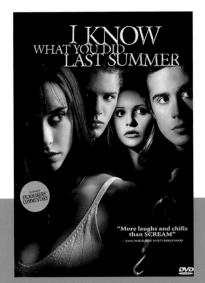

I Know What You Did Last Summer, the Movie

The 1997 movie version of Duncan's popular novel was a teen hit. Starring Jennifer Love Hewitt, Sarah Michelle Gellar, Ryan Phillipe, and Freddie Prinze, Jr., it is notable for a cast of popular young actors who went on to successful careers. Duncan notes that a missing double identity twist shifts the mystery into a horror story.

the murder were eerily similar to events in her novel *Don't Look Behind You*, which came out only a month before Kaitlyn's death. After the murder of her daughter, she found it difficult to write young adult fiction for several years. She finally returned to the form with *Gallows Hill*, a novel about a high school student whose classmates suspect her of being a witch.

Several of Lois Duncan's books have been made into feature and television films, including *I Know What You Did Last Summer* and *Killing Mr. Griffin*. In 1992 she was honored with the Margaret A. Edwards Award for Outstanding Literature for Young Adults.

p.21

p.339

– Amy Sisson

Kaitlyn Arquette

Lois Duncan's daughter, Kaitlyn Arquette was gunned down on July 16, 1989, a Sunday evening, while driving home from a friend's house in Albuquerque, New Mexico. The police claimed it was a random shooting, but Kaitlyn's parents felt otherwise. They established the New Mexico Justice Project to help families of homicide victims gain support for investigations. They also set up www.realcrimes.com as a place where victims can call attention to investigations they feel the police have suppressed. As of June of 2004, the mystery of Kaitlyn's murder still remained unsolved.

Thomas J. Dygard

Born: August 10, 1931; Little Rock, Arkansas
Died: September 30, 1996; Hazelton, Pennsylvania

Thomas J. Dygard's books typically depict adolescent males, who, in attempting to achieve their goals, encounter additional obstacles and are forced to rethink those goals. Faced with problems above and beyond those they initially encounter, Dygard's characters look toward adulthood by realizing the need to make careful and important decisions.

Dygard grew up in Arkansas, passionately interested in reading, writing, and sports. His work on his high school paper led to an internship as sportswriter with the *Arkansas Gazette*, for which he continued to write while he was earning his bachelor's degree at the University of Arkansas in his hometown of Little Rock. After graduating, he accepted a job with the **Associated Press**. Over several decades, this job took him around the world. Dygard and his wife, Patricia Redditt, whom he married in 1951, traveled to more than thirty countries.

In 1977, at the age of forty-six, Dygard accomplished another of his childhood dreams: publication of his first sports novel, *Running Scared*. This book established Dygard's stock situation: a talented athlete who must confront his own personal demons in order to play well. In his second novel, *Winning Kicker*, Dygard moved into the area of girl athletes and sexism in sports, while his third book returned to a basketball player whose success is threatened by his personality problems. Although a few of Dy-

> **.218**

TITLES

Running Scared, 1977

Winning Kicker, 1978

Outside Shooter, 1979

Point Spread, 1980

Quarterback Walk-On, 1982

Tournament Upstart, 1984

Wilderness Peril, 1985

Halfback Tough, 1986

The Rookie Arrives, 1988

Forward Pass, 1989

Backfield Package, 1992

Game Plan, 1993

Infield Hit, 1995

The Rebounder, 1996

Running Wild, 1996

River Danger, 1998

Second Stringer, 1998

gard's characters become aware that continued involvement in sports is not for them, all of them achieve self-esteem through facing their problems.

Dygard's novels go beyond the pursuit of sports, focusing on the decision-making that is required of teenagers. Dygard provides insights into the insecurities that many young people feel. The main character in *Halfback Tough* feels like an outsider in a new school and believes that his teammates are snubbing him because of his reputation as a troublemaker. Painful feelings of loneliness and confusion plague several of Dygard's characters. In *The Rebounder*, the main character, an athletic six-foot-six transfer student refuses to play basketball for his school because he once accidentally injured an opponent during a game. In *Backfield Package*, a talented quarterback is recruited by a first-rate college, destroying the plans he and his friends had made to continue their football careers together.

Dygard has also written two nonsports adventure stories. Both *Wilderness Peril* and *River Danger* depict young characters whose camping trips suddenly take dangerous turns. Unexpected occurrences and frightening events test their ingenuity, loyalty and decision-making.

Thomas Dygard's seventeen books reflect his lifelong love of sports. His lifelike characters and sit-

Associated Press (AP)

The AP is the largest news organization in the world, with some 240 news bureaus in more than 120 countries. It supplies news stories, photos, graphics, and audiovisual feeds that are transmitted to people through newspapers, radio, television, and the Internet. It is a not-for-profit cooperative owned by some 1,700 member news services.

Child Study Association of America

The CSAA was founded in 1888 as the Society for the Study of Child Nature. It was originally a discussion group for mothers, but under the direction of editor Sidonie Gruenberg it became an important national voice for opinions on child rearing. The name was changed in 1912 to the Federation for Child Study, and again in 1924 to the Child Study Association of America. In 1973, it merged with Wel-Met, Inc., another non-profit organization, which was founded in 1935 by the Metropolitan League of Jewish Community Associations to operate country camps for city children.

uations along with his fast-paced play-by-play of sporting events combine to produce exciting, realistic dilemmas of high-school athletes. He received several awards for **Books for the Teen Age** from p.156 the **New York Public Library** and was given the Child Study Association of America's **Children's Books of the Year** award in 1987. p.219

– Mary Hurd

Walter Dumaux Edmonds

Born: July 14, 1903; Boonville, New York
Died: January 24, 1998; Concord, Massachusetts

Walter D. Edmonds wrote more than thirty books and many short stories. Although many consider him as primarily a writer for young adults, he himself said that he wrote only three of his books for juvenile readers; younger readers themselves have laid claim to his other books. Edmonds set all but one of his books in New York, mostly in the region around the Erie Canal, where he grew up. In 1995, when he was more than ninety years old, he published *Tales My Father Never Told*, a poignant memoir about his youth. p.221

Born in upstate New York, Edmonds was educated at schools in New York City, New Hampshire, and Connecticut, and he graduated from Harvard University. During his junior year in college, he published an article on the Erie Canal that became the first of his works about New York's great inland waterway. By 1927 he had published sixteen stories in magazines and decided to write a book. The result was his first adult novel, *Rome Haul* (1929).

Edmonds's books span about 125 years of American history, from the time of the American Revolution through the early twentieth century. He always emphasized historical accuracy. His style was conservative, organized chronologically, and narrated in the third-person. Edmonds called his works neither fiction nor history but "chronicles of life."

Edmonds's best-known book is *Drums Along the Mohawk*, which was made into a popular film in 1939. This story is set in New York's Mohawk River

Valley during the American Revolution. It centers on a young married couple, Lana and Gil Martin, who are trying to build a home in the midst of fighting among American patriots, British loyalists, and local Indians. *In the Hands of the Senecas*, which Edmonds wrote a decade later, is a sequel. Both books provide a realistic view of the difficulties of life at that time and give a sympathetic view of Native Americans.

The Matchlock Gun is set in the same region during the **French and Indian War** of the mid-eighteenth century. In this story, a ten-year-old boy saves his mother and sister from an Indian raid by using an old Spanish matchlock gun that his father has left behind while he is on a patrol. In *Bert Breen's Barn*, a story for younger readers, a young boy falls in love with an old barn that is rumored to contain a treasure, and tries to become its owner.

p.222

Erie Canal

In the early 1800's, farmers and merchants in the western settlements of the U.S. had difficulty shipping their goods to the East Coast. The most common shipping route was down the Ohio and Mississippi rivers to New Orleans and from there to the East Coast. Between 1817 and 1825, a 363-mile canal was built connecting Albany, New York, on the Hudson River, with Buffalo, New York, on Lake Erie. The success of the Erie Canal led to the building of other canals and systems of transport, and East Coast cities could then compete with one another for their share of the western trade.

WALTER DUMAUX EDMONDS

French and Indian War

In addition to the original thirteen colonies, the British claimed the territory that is now Northern Canada. The French claimed a huge section stretching from New Orleans in the south to what is now Montana in the northwest and Quebec in the northeast. The French built forts along the Mississippi River to defend their territory. The territory along the Ohio River, which flows southwest along the western frontier of Pennsylvania and Virginia, was claimed by both the British and the French. In 1754, General George Washington led British troops to build a fort in the territory but found the French already there. The British were defeated in the subsequent battle. Both parties sought the help of Indians, and in 1759 the decisive battle was fought in Quebec. The British defeated the French and then took Montreal in 1760 as well. In the Treaty of Paris, 1763, the French gave up their claim to all French lands east of the Mississippi, including New Orleans.

Many organizations have honored Walter Edmonds's writings. The American Library Association awarded him the Newbery Medal for *The Matchlock Gun*. *Bert Breen's Barn* won the **Christopher Award** and the **National Book Award** for Children's Books. The Boys' Clubs of America granted Edmonds their book award for *Hound Dog Moses and the Promised Land*. Edmonds also received honorary degrees from Union College, Rutgers University, and Colgate University.

– Anita Price Davis

 p.45

p.10?

p.12?

p.20?

Nancy Farmer

Born: July 9, 1941; Phoenix, Arizona

www.peacecorpsonline.org/messages/
messages/467/2016734.html

Nancy Farmer's novels for young adults feature harrowing but delightful adventures in exotic settings. Some are futuristic, filled with flying cars, atomic mutations, clones, and strange humanoids. Some are set in Africa (including one futuristic story) and in these, characters commune with traditional African spirits. In all her books, characters embark on spiritual as well as physical quests.

Farmer was born in Arizona and regards her upbringing in a hotel near the Arizona-**New Mexico** border as good preparation for her writing. At the age of nine, she began working at the hotel desk and hearing the stories of traveling circus performers, rodeo riders, and railroad workers. After graduating from Reed College in Oregon, she joined the **Peace Corps**, learned Hindi, and went to India as a teacher. Later she studied chemistry, and eventually moved to Mozambique, then Zimbabwe, where she worked as a lab technician and met her future husband, Harold Farmer, who taught English at the local university.

Farmer's first two novels for young adults are set in southern Africa. In *The Ear, the Eye, and the Arm*, the three children of Zimbabwe's military chief in the year 2194 decide to visit the big city but are kidnapped by an elephantine woman who imprisons them in a toxic dump. The frantic parents hire three young detectives named Ear, Eye, and Arm, who

 p.24

p.224

Peace Corps

In 1960, then-Senator John F. Kennedy challenged students at the University of Michigan to serve their country in the cause of peace by living and working in developing countries. Out of his challenge, the Peace Corps was born as a federal government agency dedicated to world peace and friendship. Since its beginning, more than 170,000 volunteers have worked in some 136 host countries helping to improve agricultural methods, preserve the environment, provide health education, and introduce information technology.

have special abilities resulting from nuclear mutations. As the children escape and are recaptured, they slip into a tribal village walled off from the modern world and inhabited by **shamans**, p.336 witches, spirits, and superstitious villagers When they escape, they rescue a baby who villagers believe carries a curse.

In *A Girl Named Disaster*, spirits fill an even larger role for the main character, Nhamo, who talks frequently with her dead mother and an array of other colorful spirits. At the age of eleven, Nhamo sets out on a perilous journey from Mozambique to Zimbabwe to find her father and to flee an arranged marriage with a cruel man. Nhamo proves herself a brave soul, both in her dangerous journey and in her coping with the surprising results of her quest.

Farmer set *The House of the Scorpion* in the imaginary future country of Opium, a nation formed after years of United States-Mexico border wars. The new country's economy is based on **opium** pro- p.225 duction; the work is overseen by drug lords and performed by humanoids with computer chips in their brains. Matteo, a fourteen-year-old clone of a drug overlord, ultimately escapes Opium, but returns to help heal the country. As with *The Ear, the Eye, and the Arm*, this novel explores the cultural implications of technology run amok.

p.102
Nancy Farmer's many writing honors include **Newbery** and Golden Kite Honor Book awards for *The Ear, the Eye, and the Arm*; **Newbery Honor Book** and American Library Association **Best Book for Young Adults** for *A Girl Named Disaster*, which was also a nominee for the **National Book Award**; and a National Book Award and an ALA **Best Book for Young Adults** award for *The House of the Scorpion*.
p.111

p.480

p.45

p.122

– Jan Allister

Opium

Opium is a substance collected from the seed pods of the opium poppy. It is the source of the drugs morphine, codeine, and heroin. The first two drugs are used in medicine, morphine as a painkiller and codeine for coughs. However, medical use is watched carefully as overuse of these drugs can cause addiction. Heroin is an illegal substance that is highly addictive and causes a feeling of calm and well being.

Afghanistan is one of the world's biggest producers of opium, and officials struggle to keep poor rural farmers from growing crops of opium poppies to sell to illegal drug lords.

Howard Fast

Born: November 11, 1914; New York, New York
Died: March 12, 2003; Old Greenwich, Connecticut

www.trussel.com/f_how.htm

Most of **Howard Fast**'s characters undergo realistic experiences that lead them to new realizations about America's heritage. His characters are mostly men who participate in or observe dramatic moments in history and explore the price of freedom. Lifelike characters and brisk, action-packed narratives are trademarks of Fast's novels. Although he did not always write his books specifically for young readers, his books have entertained young adults for decades.

The grandson of Ukrainian immigrants to the United States, Fast grew up in New York City in a family that struggled to make ends meet. From the age of ten, he worked at odd jobs. While working in the **New York Public Library** as a teenager, he p.156 found time to pursue his passion—writing. At the age of seventeen, he sold his first story and soon began to write full time. In 1937, he married Bette Cohen, a painter and sculptor; they had two children.

At the beginning of World War II, Fast was at the height of his popularity. From his own experiences with anti-Semitism and extreme poverty, he developed a strong social conscience. He was drawn to downtrod-

Communist Party

Communist Party, USA
www.cpusa.org

The Communist Party of the United States of America was founded following the Bolshevik Revolution in Russia. It was based on the ideas of Karl Marx and Friedrich Engels expressed in *The Communist Manifesto* and Marx's work *Das Kapital*. The basis of communism lies in the belief that throughout history, the working class has been taken advantage of by the upper classes. It supports transfer of power to the workers. The party attracted many members during the Great Depression, when millions of workers could not find jobs and lived in poverty. During the Cold War, which began following World War II and lasted until the fall of the Soviet Union in 1991, there was strong anticommunist feeling in the U.S.

den and oppressed peoples and began to write about them. In 1941 he wrote *The Last Frontier*, a story of the defiant journey of the northern Cheyenne Indians from their Oklahoma **Reservation** to Montana. p.725 Although told from the point of view of the white men, the novel offers a fresh look at the Cheyenne, heroic victims of persecution, who valued freedom more than their lives.

In 1943 Fast wrote *Citizen Tom Paine*, a fictionalized biography of a controversial eighteenth century figure, whom he portrays vividly as a hero who fought during the American Revolution for freedom of the mind. Following this somewhat radical depiction of Paine, Fast joined the **Communist Party**, whose beliefs were reflected in his life and writing p.227 for the next thirteen years. Still concerned with social oppression, Fast wrote his first protest novel, *Freedom Road*, to criticize racial inequity in American society. Its **protagonist** is Gideon Jackson, a p.233 former slave who becomes a Congressman after the Civil War but is eventually killed by the **Ku Klux Klan**. Fast then shifted his interest from the Ameri- p.330 can Reconstruction era to ancient **Roman history**. p.530 His popular and controversial novel *Spartacus* is named after the historical leader of an unsuccessful

Blacklisting

Blacklisting is when individuals or groups are punished or denied employment because of their beliefs or membership in certain groups. It reached its height during the Cold War in the U.S. In the 1950's, the House Committee on Un-American Activities targeted Hollywood because movies had the potential to reach so many people. Eventually 212 people were barred from working in Hollywood because of their assumed affiliation with the Communist Party.

slave revolt, which to Fast represented the struggles of all oppressed people against their inhuman masters.

Because of his communist ties, Howard Fast was jailed for three months and found himself **blacklisted**. For several years no publishing house would accept his manuscripts. Consequently, he wrote twenty light suspense novels using the pen name of E. V. Cunningham. In 1957 he publicly recanted his belief in communism and returned to writing about the American Revolutionary period. Four years later he published *April Morning*, a historical novel that became standard reading for students in public schools for many years. It is a vivid account of a fifteen-year-old's coming of age during the Battle of Lexington on April 19, 1775. In all, Fast wrote more than fifty books that include novels, plays and nonfiction. Many of his books have been made into films.

– Mary Hurd

p.228

p.620

p.117

William Faulkner

Born: September 25, 1897; New Albany, Mississippi
Died: July 6, 1962; Byhalia, Mississippi

www.mcsr.olemiss.edu/~egjbp/faulkner/faulkner.html

William Faulkner is generally recognized as one of America's greatest writers, but little of what he wrote is aimed specifically at young adult readers. His most accessible works for younger readers are two of his short stories, "The Bear," which is part of *Go Down, Moses*, and "Barn Burning," which won an **O. Henry Award**. Both are coming-of-age stories. Among other Faulkner works that are read by teenagers are *The Sound and the Fury* (1929), *As I Lay Dying* (1930), and *A Fable* (1954). *The Unvanquished* (1938), a collection of seven short stories that Faulkner turned into a novel about the Sartoris family is also popular among young adults.

Born William Cuthbert Falkner, the oldest of the four sons of Murry and Maud Butler Falkner (he added the "u" to his name during the 1920's), Faulkner spent his entire life in Mississippi and became renowned for a series of novels that focus on the development of the American South as depicted in his mythical Mississippi county of Yoknapatawpha. He is centrally concerned with the exploitation of the land worked by underpaid former slaves and **tenant farmers** raising **cotton**, the region's major cash crop. He published his first book, *Soldiers' Pay*, in 1926, following it in the next decade with five more novels and a procession of short stories. Ever pressed for money, he

TITLES

"Barn Burning," 1939

"The Bear" in *Go Down, Moses and Other Stories*, 1942

The Reivers, 1962

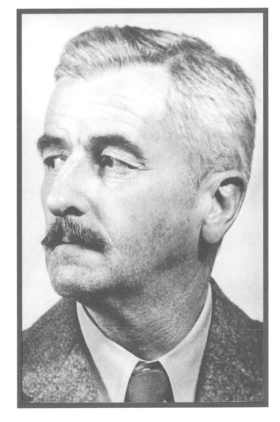

.230
.291

worked intermittently in Hollywood's film industry.

Faulkner's prize-winning "Barn Burning" is a story of the inner conflict that Sarty Snopes, a ten-year-old boy, endures as he is torn between testifying for his father, an arsonist, and revealing what he knows. His father's habitual arson crimes force the family to relocate frequently. Early in the story, Sarty is prepared to testify on his father's behalf, although he knows that his testimony will be untruthful. Later, Sarty realizes that his father is about to torch a plantation. Suffering severe misgivings about being disloyal to his father, he finally warns the owner of his father's plan and, in doing so, destroys his family's future.

"The Bear" is among the seven stories that make up *Go Down, Moses*. Faulkner intended that this collection be read collectively as a novel that traces the family history of the McCaslins, prominent citizens of Yoknapatawpha County, from their arrival there in the early 1800's to the 1940's. "The Bear," focusing on young Ike McCaslin, recounts the lad's initiation into manhood during a ritualistic hunt

Tenant Farmer

A tenant farmer does not own the land he farms. He pays the landlord either cash or a share of the crops he harvests. When slavery was abolished and cotton farmers lost ownership of the slaves who worked the fields, they often leased their land to a tenant farmer or a sharecropper. A sharecropper received credit for seed, tools, housing, and other supplies and repaid this debt with the earnings from a portion of the resulting crops. A sharecropper often did not earn enough from his share of the crops to repay his debt and became deeper in debt to the landlord. The Southern Tenant Farmer's Union was an interracial organization founded in 1935 by sharecroppers to seek government aid for sharecroppers and tenant farmers during the Great Depression. This racially integrated group was a major achievement in the still highly segregated American South.

Nobel Prize in Literature

Alfred Nobel, a Swede who invented dynamite and who was an entrepreneur and philan-thropist, stipulated in his will in 1895 that one of five annual awards be given in the field of literature to "the person whose work shall have produced in the field of literature the most outstanding work of an ideal tendency" and that the prize be distributed by the Academy in Stockholm. This vague qualification has been interpreted by the Academy to honor an author for his or her entire produc-tion rather than a specific work, although on some occasions a specific work has been mentioned. The Nobel is the ultimate liter-ary prize.

for the legendary bear called Old Ben. Through this experience, Ike learns and accepts his place in na-ture and in society.

In 1949 William Faulkner became the fourth American writer to receive the Nobel Prize in Lit-erature. In his acceptance speech for the award, p.231 Faulkner noted his lifelong concern with the prob-lems of the human heart in conflict with itself. He re-vealed that universals such as love, honor, pity, pride, compassion, and sacrifice consistently en-gaged him artistically.

– R. Baird Shuman

Carol Fenner

Born: September 30, 1929; Almond, New York
Died: February 16, 2002; Battle Creek, Michigan

Carol Fenner is best known for her reality-based stories of well-drawn African American pro-tagonists struggling to overcome the obstacles that face all children as they grow up. Her books deftly balance three-dimensional characters and fast-paced plots.

p.233

Fenner achieved success as both a writer and an **illustrator** but started her career as an actor in plays, commercials, and films. She also worked in an **advertising agency** before publishing her first pic-ture book for young children in 1963. As a child, she began composing poems before she could write, so her mother recorded her words for her. She also be-gan drawing at an early age and continued to de-velop her skills in her adult life, although she re-ceived no formal training in either creative writing or art. Her role model was her aunt, Phyllis Fenner, a school **librarian** renowned for her **storytelling**, who wrote more than fifty books. Fenner's aunt in-stilled in her a love of poetry and an appreciation for the forms and rhythms of language.

p.38

p.657

p.35

p.234

In *The Skates of Uncle Richard* an African American girl, Marsha, dreams of becoming a cham-pion figure skater. However, her hopes for beautiful new skates are dashed when she receives hand-me-down hockey skates from her uncle. She overcomes her disappointment, and her skills improve as she comes to appreciate both her own talents and the value of her uncle's help.

Randall's Wall is the story of a fifth-grade boy, Randall, who lives with a father who abuses him and a mother who ignores him. His home lacks running water, so his personal hygiene is poor, and other children reject him. In self-defense, he erects a psychological wall against emotional pain, only to have it breached by a girl whom he saves from a bully. She helps him uncover and reveal his talent for art.

Yolanda's Genius tells the story of an overweight but intelligent, fifth-grade girl, who moves from the inner city to a Chicago suburb after a violent incident at her school. A child of the streets, Yolanda is accustomed to big-city ways, so the customs of the suburbs elude her. She decides that Andrew, her "slow-learner" younger brother, who seldom speaks and cannot read, is in fact a musical prodigy. While struggling to make friends at school, Yolanda reveals that genius comes in many forms. Fenner has said her husband's passion for music inspired this book.

Fenner's final book, *The King of Dragons*, tells the story of a **homeless** boy, Ian, and his father. The pair find shelter in an abandoned city courthouse, only to have their haven disrupted by the arrival of an exhibit of kites and the museum crew that is setting it up. Hungry for knowledge, Ian learns everything he can about the kites and masquerades as a museum guide. Ian's father, a **Vietnam War** veteran, behaves at times irrationally, but his behavior becomes more comprehensible as Ian learns about the events and effects of the Vietnam War.

p.732

p.90

Protagonist

A protagonist in Greek drama was the first actor who played a leading role. However, that term has now come to mean the most important character, usually a hero or heroine, in a play or a story. It is the character we most care about and around whom the action of the story is built.

National Storytelling Network

The National Storytelling Network (NSN) is an organization dedicated to advancing the art of storytelling. Storytelling can take place anywhere that interested listeners choose to gather. The classroom, the library, auditoriums, and even coffee houses or club meetings provide opportunities for storytellers to perform. Oral storytelling is how stories were communicated before written language. Early literature, such as the ancient Greek Homer's *Illiad* and *The Odyssey*, is based on stories that were told rather than read. Homer gave these stories a poetic form. The British legend of King Arthur and the Knights of the Round Table also traces its roots to oral tradition. NSN provides its members with conferences and additional resources to keep the art of storytelling alive.

Carol Fenner's writing honors include the **Coretta Scott King Award** for *The Skates of Uncle Richard*, which was adapted for television by Children's Television International. *Yolanda's Genius* received a **Newbery Honor Book** award and was named a **Notable Children's Book** by the **American Library Association**.

p.66

p.102

p.45

– Faith Hickman Brynie

Jean Ferris

Born: January 24, 1939; Fort Leavenworth, Kansas

www.jeanferris.com

Jean Ferris understands that adolescence is a time of change and challenge, so she writes novels about coping with realistic teenage problems. She draws upon her personal experiences, interviews with teenagers, and the experiences of her two daughters to bring authenticity to her fictional characters. Although she started writing as a child, she initially had no ambition to make writing her career. Her husband's urging to clean out all of her papers in their house motivated her to submit a book for publication. She was surprised when *Amen, Moses Gardenia*, a story about a **teenage girl's depression** and attempted suicide, was accepted.

p.302

Life-threatening illness and relationships forge the plot in two of Ferris's novels: *The Stainless Steel Rule* and *Invincible Summer*. Three girls are best friends until handsome Nick pulls Mary away in *The Stainless Steel Rule*. Nick's influence grows so strong that he convinces Mary that she does not need her friends or insulin for her **diabetes**. Mary slips into a coma. When she recovers, she realizes that Fran and Kitty are her true friends. *Invincible Summer*, which received wide critical acclaim, is a celebration of life. Rick and his girlfriend, Robin, both have **leukemia**. They decide to experience as much of life as they possibly can before Rick becomes too ill to do anything.

p.236

p.237

Ferris used a male **protagonist** in *Across the Grain*. In this story, seventeen-year-old Will must move to California with his older sister, Paige. When Paige becomes the manager of a small restaurant,

p.233

TITLES

Amen, Moses Gardenia, 1983

The Stainless Steel Rule, 1986

Invincible Summer, 1987

Across the Grain, 1990

All That Glitters, 1996

Bad, 1998

Love Among the Walnuts, 1998

Eight Seconds, 2000

Of Sound Mind, 2001

Once Upon a Marigold, 2002

Will works with her, and one of their regular customers, Sam, becomes a father-figure to him. A story of love and friendship, this book was selected by the American Library Association as a **Best Book for Young Adults** (1992). A scuba diving adventure brings a father and son closer in *All That Glitters*.

When Ferris visited the Girls' Rehabilitation Facility (GRC) in her hometown of San Diego, California, to share *All That Glitters*, the teenage girls asked her to write a novel about them. This resulted in *Bad*. In this book, sixteen-year-old Dallas is persuaded by her friends to join them in robbing a convenience store, and she is the only one caught. Her father thinks she needs to learn a lesson, so she is sentenced to six months in the GRC. There Dallas interacts with "bad" girls and realizes that she made a mistake by giving in to peer pressure. When she leaves the facility, she chooses to make a clean break with her past and moves into a group home rather

p.45

Diabetes

Diabetes is a hormone disorder where the body does not produce enough insulin to support the proper levels of blood sugar. A diabetic has enough sugar in the blood, but without insulin the sugar cannot reach the cells that need it for energy. Glucose, the simplest form of sugar, is the main source of energy for many vital functions. Without glucose, cells starve and tissues begin to break down. Diabetics must test their glucose levels throughout the day and may require insulin injections to regulate the blood sugar levels.

Leukemia

Leukemia is a form of cancer characterized by the abnormal increase of white blood cells in the body's tissues and blood. While there are no tumors as with other cancers, the cancerous white blood cells restrict the development of new blood cells. The patient will become weak because there are not enough oxygen-carrying red blood cells and may bleed easily because there are not enough platelets. Treatment for leukemia involves chemotherapy or bone marrow transplant, both very aggressive treatments. Many patients will experience remission, or the absence of cancer cells, following treatment. Leukemia can be cured in many patients at a higher level than many other cancers.

than return to her unsupportive father.

Ferris interjects an element of mystery into *Love Among the Walnuts*. Sandy and his wealthy family are targeted by his greedy uncles who want the family fortune. With the help of the butler and a sympathetic nurse from the asylum next door, Sandy tends to his family and foils the plot.

In all her books, Jean Ferris tries to leave her readers with hope, and she frequently shares her work directly with her fans by speaking at conferences. Her many honors include American Library Association **Best Books for Young Adults** awards for *Love Among the Walnuts*, *Bad*, *Eight Seconds*, *Of Sound Mind*, and *Once Upon a Marigold*.

– Kay Moore

F. Scott Fitzgerald

Born: September 24, 1896; St. Paul, Minnesota
Died: December 21, 1940; Hollywood, California

www.fitzgeraldsociety.org

TITLE

The Great Gatsby, 1925

F. Scott Fitzgerald is one of America's finest authors. Of the five novels and several volumes of short stories that he produced during his relatively brief life, the book most often read in high schools and colleges is *The Great Gatsby*. This novel is filled with both joy and tragedy. Its narrator, Nick Carraway, uses the first-person point of view to tell about the year (presumably 1920) in which he lives in New York. There he meets his cousin, Daisy, her husband, the brutish Tom Buchanan, and the young man who has adored Daisy from afar for many years, the mysterious Jay Gatsby.

The Buchanans and their friends represent the "idle rich." Gatsby, however, worked his way up from a dirt-poor background, eventually making his fortune selling liquor illegally during the **Prohibition** era in order to purchase a mansion near Daisy's. Daisy and her friends are shallow, snobbish socialites who spend all their time partying; they contribute little to society. Although Gatsby has earned his money illegally, he possesses a vision of what America should be and has a steadfast determination to replace the sordid facts of his own past with beauty. These qualities make him lovable and "great."

p.239

Young people enjoy *The Great Gatsby* for many reasons. For one thing, it is simply and beautifully written; Fitzgerald's prose is often poetic. For another, the images he employs are easy to understand. Most famous are his use of color, as in the green light on Daisy's dock that Gatsby gazes at from his lawn; the "valley of ashes" that lies between the villages of East Egg (where the Buchanans live) and West Egg (where Nick and Gatsby live); and the advertising billboard featuring the eyes of "Dr. Eckleburg," which most critics agree represents the absence of God from this society.

Fitzgerald seduces the reader with the glitter of high society as Nick moves to the **Long Island** Sound and rents a house surrounded by mansions. Both Tom, and Daisy's friend Jordan Baker, are athletes; Daisy is a beautiful "Golden Girl." Nick goes from one party to another, first at Daisy's home, then at the apartment of Tom's mistress, then at Gatsby's house. However, Nick reveals his disgust with these people who tell lies, cheat on each other, and care for nobody but themselves. The feeling

Prohibition

On January 16, 1920, the Eighteenth Amendment to the constitution became law. It gave the federal government the right to control liquor, previously under state and local control. Sale, transport, or import of alcoholic beverages was banned in the U.S. This quickly led to "bootlegging" (the illegal sale of liquor), and a new industry was born. Rather than discourage the drinking of liquor, this ban actually encouraged people to drink. By 1929, President Hoover appointed a commission to investigate law enforcement and liquor. Its findings confirmed that prohibition had encouraged a disrespect for the law. By December 5, 1933, the Twenty-first Amendment repealed prohibition.

of an imminent crash builds, and it occurs both metaphorically and literally in a car accident which kills Tom's mistress, Myrtle. A series of misunderstandings climaxes with the murder of Jay Gatsby.

The story is a quick read and, from the very beginning, poignant and exciting. Because the characters are so universal, readers can always relate to them or criticize them. Students enjoy discussing such themes as appearances versus reality, the conflict between wealthy and poor, and the richness of hope, wonder, dream and disappointment as Jay Gatsby lives them and as Fitzgerald heartbreakingly portrays them.

The Great Gatsby has been adapted as a **film** four times; the two best versions star Alan Ladd (1949) and Robert Redford (1974) as Gatsby.

p.24

– Fiona Kelleghan

The Great Gatsby, the Movie

The 1970 film version of *The Great Gatsby* suffers the usual fate of movies derived from classic books or stories. It cannot replicate the unique experience that a reader has with a book. With a cast led by Robert Redford as Jay Gatsby, and Mia Farrow as Daisy, and with a screenplay by Francis Ford Coppola of *Godfather* fame, viewers were satisfied with a movie featuring beautiful sets and costumes. The reading experience is better than the viewing.

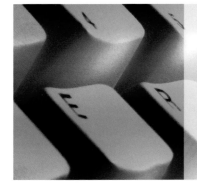

Paul Fleischman

Born: September 5, 1952; Monterey, California

www.paulfleischman.net

Polyphony—a musical term for a piece in which several independent melodies blend together—is a word that aptly describes the work of author **Paul Fleischman**. He is well known for his children's poetry collections *Joyful Noise: Poems for Two Voices* (1988) and *I Am Phoenix* (1985), which developed the idea of poetry as a duet for voices. He has also adapted the concept of multiple voices to a wide range of works, including picture books, nonfiction, and young adult novels. His novels for young adult readers experiment with multiple narrators and multiple points of view, which weave through his books like the voices in a polyphonic musical work by the seventeenth century German composer Johann Sebastian Bach. Experimentation with words, a fascination with history, and a tendency to break the boundaries of genre between poetry, nonfiction, theater, and fiction are the hallmarks of much of Paul Fleischman's work.

Fleischman was born in Monterey, California, the son of the well-known and award-winning children's book author Sid Fleischman. His father influenced him, though perhaps indirectly, to pursue a career in writing. Fleischman attended the University of California at Berkeley and graduated from the University of **New Mexico**. He gave little thought to a writing career until his graduation and then realized that such a future was a real possibility. He had been preparing for it all his life by watching his father work and through his own interest in music.

p.24

TITLES

The Half-a-Moon Inn, 1980

Graven Images, 1982

Path of the Pale Horse, 1983

Rear-View Mirrors, 1986

Saturnalia, 1990

Bull Run, 1993

A Fate Totally Worse than Death, 1995

Seedfolks, 1997

Whirligig, 1998

Mind's Eye, 1999

Seek, 2001

Breakout, 2003

Performance Art

This avant-garde form of art can take place in the theater, on the streets, before the camera, in an art gallery, or almost anywhere you can imagine. It might be a person talking without a script, which is called improvising. It might also be an artist posting signs or images at public places throughout the city or drawing symbols in chalk on the sidewalk. What all these types of art have in common is the sense of the artist thumbing his or her nose at established conventions or rules. Performance art is often a controversial statement about society and culture.

All of Fleischman's prose stresses the importance of words and their sounds. Fleischman often writes what might be considered prose poems, in which combinations of sounds are as important as plot and character. His novels *Seedfolks* and *Whirligig* rely on multiple narrators, each with a distinctive voice. *Whirligig* tells the story of a boy who accidentally causes the death of classmate and promises to atone for his sin by traveling to the four corners of the country to plant whirligigs (wind toys) as tokens of his repentance.

Two other novels, *Mind's Eye* and *Seek*, experiment with the boundaries between drama and fiction by having the burden of each story emerge through dialogue, music, radio broadcasts, and a combination of prose and poetry. *Mind's Eye* develops the relationship between a teenager with a disability and an elderly woman, while *Seek* features a teenage boy searching for the father who abandoned him. Fleischman's work might almost be characterized as **performance art**, as it relies greatly on the idea of the power of the spoken word and the mixing of genres.

p.242

Fleischman's novels also show a respect for and a fascination with the past. *Saturnalia*, which is set in seventeenth century Boston, and *Bull Run*, featuring the voices of sixteen observers of that important Civil War battle, revive the milieu of the past and the voices and dialects of the people who lived then. Two of Fleischman's short story collections, *Graven Images* and *The Half-a-Moon Inn* pay homage to nineteenth century writers Edgar Allan Poe and Nathaniel Hawthorne in both content and style.

p.243

Paul Fleischman is one of the most frequently honored writers of books for young readers. His many awards include a **Newbery Medal** for *Joyful Noise*. He has also received four American Library Association **Best Books for Young Adults** awards, the Scott O'Dell Award for Historical Fiction for *Bull Run*, and numerous Boston Globe-Horn Honor Book and Golden Kite Honor Book awards.

p.102
p.45
p.480
p.51
p.111
p.747

– Ann M. Cameron

Battle of Bull Run

In 1861, Union and Confederate soldiers met in Northern Virginia to clash in the first major battle of the Civil War. Also known as the First Battle of Manassas, Bull Run was the largest battle fought at that time in North America. The North marched a poorly trained army of 35,000 men from Washington, D.C., toward Richmond, Virginia, which had been named the Confederate capital. The Northern troops were overwhelmed by the fresh Confederate troops, who had been sent to the area by railroad. However, while the Confederate troops were victorious, they were too exhausted and disorganized to move on to Washington. The North learned from its defeat and began serious training of troops and supply preparation for future battles.

Esther Forbes

Born: June 28, 1891; Westboro, Massachusetts
Died: August 12, 1967; Worcester, Massachusetts

www.wpi.edu/Academics/Library/Archives/WAuthors/
   forbes/

The inspiration for **Esther Forbes**'s novel *Johnny Tremain*, one of the most acclaimed young adult books of modern times, first entered her mind when she was doing research for a nonfiction book on the Revolutionary War hero Paul Revere. She read a historical account saying that a young messenger boy on horseback first brought word to Revere about a crucial movement of British troops in April, 1775. The boy, whose name was lost to history, was transformed in Forbes's imagination into the title character of *Johnny Tremain*. The novel won a **Newbery Medal** and has remained p.10: continuously in print since its publication. The Walt Disney Company made a film version of *Johnny Tremain* in 1957, and Forbes rode to the film's Boston premiere in a Disney limousine.

The fifth of sixth children born to a Massachusetts family, Forbes gained an early familiarity with the worlds of education, history, and writing. Her father was a college professor who later became a lawyer, and her mother was a writer and historian who had traveled widely throughout the United States before her marriage. Despite these advantages Forbes did not perform well in

Dyslexia

Dyslexia is a reading disability in individuals who are of average or above-average intelligence. It is thought to be caused by brain damage or brain dysfunction. It frustrates those children who are dyslexic, can damage their self image, and can decrease their future contribution to society as adults if left unrecognized or untreated. Treatment usually begins in school in special-education classes where teachers work with individual students who have reading disabilities. The support of parents is especially important. Dyslexic individuals are often highly creative and personally successful. Famous dyslexics include: *Actors and entertainers*, Tom Cruise, Robin Williams, Whoopi Goldberg, Jay Leno; *inventor*, Thomas Edison; *scientist*, Albert Einstein; *athletes*, Nolan Ryan, Muhammad Ali, and Magic Johnson; *U.S. presidents*, George Washington and John F. Kennedy; *filmmaker*, Walt Disney; and *musicians*, Cher and John Lennon.

school, partly because of vision problems and dyslexia. She displayed an early talent for storytelling, but when she turned in a short story for a class assignment the teacher accused her of plagiarizing the work. Esther vowed never to share her stories with teachers again.

Later, while studying at the University of Wisconsin, Forbes was encouraged by a writing teacher. That led her to publish "Breakneck Hill" in a literary magazine, and the story won an **O. Henry Prize** for short fiction. Forbes's first novel, *O Genteel Lady!*, was a selection of the Book-of-the-Month Club and her career was off to a promising start.

 Before the publication of *Johnny Tremain*, historical fiction was typically written from the points of view of the leading figures of historical eras. Forbes took a different approach, telling the story of the Revolutionary War through the experiences of Johnny, a fourteen-year-old apprentice silversmith who is both talented and over-confident. When a serious injury cripples his hand, he has to find a new career. While delivering newspapers, he is recruited as a messenger and a spy for the Sons of

Apprentice

An apprentice is someone who enters a training program to learn how to do a job from those already qualified and working at the profession. In some countries, young adults go directly from school into apprentice programs to learn a professional skill or trade, such as cooking, retail sales, plumbing, or carpentry. Beginning in 2004, a popular reality television show called *The Apprentice* followed a group of young professionals who performed tasks for multi-millionaire and New York real estate mogul Donald Trump, with the hope of being the one selected to manage one of his many businesses.

Liberty and comes to play an important role in such history-book events as the Boston Tea Party and the Battle of Lexington. Along the way, he gets to know the early patriot leaders who would become America's Founders, such as John and Samuel Adams, John Hancock, and Paul Revere. Johnny also experiences, at first hand, the loss and pain of war at the crucial but costly battles at Lexington and Concord. He struggles with questions about the justification for war that continue to be relevant in the modern-day world.

– Carroll Dale Short

Photo Credits

Digital Stock: 24, 41, 50, 110, 342, 413, 512, 590, 612, 714

Eric Stahlbert, Sophia Smith Collection, Smith College: 553

Evan Bauer: 52

Eyewire: 485

Federal Bureau of Investigation (FBI): 161

F. R. Niglutsch: 311, 312, 530, 726

Frances M. Roberts: 141

HarperCollins: 433

Houghton Mifflin Co.: 104, 679

Howard University: 138

Hulton Archives | by Getty Images: 7, 211, 586

International Reading Association: 621

Jane Bown: 554

Jerry Bauer: 383

John Cofer: 517

Kentucky School Media Association: 438

Lambda Literary Foundation: 264

Library of Congress: 13, 14, 27, 31, 42, 47, 72, 84, 94, 97, 107, 112, 116, 129, 163, 171, 174, 187, 190, 191, 197, 209, 213, 222, 238, 239, 243, 279, 318, 319, 329, 355, 365, 386, 391, 392, 401, 428, 429, 437, 440, 450, 453, 520, 531, 559, 573, 580, 593, 653, 660, 665, 685, 689, 700, 701, 718, 728

Los Angeles Public Library: 360

Marie-Claude Aullas Bosse: 82

MGM: 285

Missouri Historical Society: 124

M. L. Marinelli: 633

Museum of Modern Art, Film Stills Archive: 93, 393, 521, 720

National Alliance for Autism Research: 704

National Archives: 165, 543, 607, 674

National Italian American Foundation: 182

National Japanese American Historical Society: 675

National Library of Australia: 635

National Library of Scotland: 353

National Museum of the American Indian: 509

National Portrait Gallery, Smithsonian Institution: 699

National Storytelling Network: 234

National Trust for Historic Preservation: 86

Norwich University: 611

Oberlin College: 615

Oklahoma Center for the Book: 276

Oxford University Press: 536

PEN American Center: 723

PhotoDisc: 36, 126, 189, 321, 327, 473, 498, 561, 662, 663

Pima Community College: 269

Psychiatric Times: 557

Random House Books: 337

Ray Grist: 121

Reed Business Information: 144

Robert Foothorap: 664

Royal Society of Literature: 261

San Francisco Museum of Modern Art: 482

Seth Kantner: 373

Society of Children's Book Writers and Illustrators: 111

The International Dyslexia Association: 245

The Nobel Foundation: 229, 280, 322, 326, 362, 649

Thomas Victor: 91

Twentieth Century Fox: 629

University of Massachusetts: 434

Western Writers of America: 335

William Foster: 715

Young Adult Library Services Association: 258

Subject Index